The Ultimate Guide To

GORGE BOULDERING

A select guide
to unique bouldering
opportunities in the
Columbia River Gorge

Gorge Bouldering Select
Copyright © 2019 East Wind Design
All rights reserved. This book is protected under copyright law and is the property of the publisher. No part of this book may be reproduced or transmitted in any form without written permission from the author and publisher.

Book Design: East Wind Design
Technical Maps and Illustrations: East Wind Design

Cover Photograph: Bouldering at *Larch Mtn Boulders*
Frontispiece images: *Larch Mtn., and High Rocks Boulders*

International Standard Book Number
ISBN-13: 978-0-9997233-2-6

Gorge Bouldering Select (GBS) v1.4
Printed in the USA

Photo credits: Mr Abbott, Mr Fields.

GORGE BOULDERING

Table of Contents

Introduction
- Climate 2
- Basic Geology 3
- Inherent Risks 4
- Using This Book 5
- Bouldering Grade Scale 5
- Star Ratings 6
- Info Symbols 6
- Gear & Supplies 7

Columbia River Gorge
- Larch Mtn Boulders 9
- Hamilton Boulders 27
- Alpenglow Boulders 39
- Empire Boulders 49
- Horsethief Butte 89

Quality Alternate Destinations
- Hunchback Boulders 105

Disclaimer

Rock climbing (and bouldering) is an inherently dangerous activity. The publisher and author of this guidebook assume no responsibility for injury or death resulting from the use of this book. This book is not intended to serve as an instructional manual and should not take the place of proper training. If you are unsure of your ability to handle any circumstances that may arise, seek professional instruction or attain the services of a professional guide.

Errors may exist in this book and we cannot be held responsible for injury or death while using this guidebook. You and you alone assume complete responsibility for your safety.

The author and publisher makes no representations or warranties, expressed or implied, of any kind regarding the contents of this guide. They make no representations or warranties, expressed or otherwise implied regarding the accuracy or reliability of this guide. The user assumes all risk associated with the use of this book and all activities contained within.

It's A Bouldering World

It's A Bouldering World

INTRODUCTION

Bouldering opportunities in the Columbia River Gorge

This Gorge Bouldering booklet brings together in one place, a specifically focused authentic select list of the best bouldering opportunities that combined make a cool core group of unique and locally popular bouldering hangouts in the Columbia River Gorge.

This booklet encapsulates that select list into a concise in-depth analysis ideal for any boulderer seeking a fast key gateway to some of our nearby favorite bouldering destinations mere miles from Portland, Oregon.

The world of regional outdoor bouldering, centered around Portland, Oregon has been a rapidly changing game, bringing new opportunities for the quest seeking, nuance-driven boulderer who is determined to tap the latest cool problems found in the sport of bouldering. This book provides a power-packed analysis of a selection of well established bouldering sites that are sure to spike your enthusiasm to a new high.

This book takes you on a tour of a core group of hotspots in the Columbia River Gorge, capturing within this book a brief set of essential tools to play the game, as well as providing you with the primary reason to be part of this growing Northwest Oregon bouldering sport. This booklet is a key solution for any travel-meister en route to other gold, and even time-crunched local-meisters who just want a core pack detailed guide to certain prime local bouldering sites.

Today's boulderer can easily maintain 12-month continuity fitness levels throughout the year thanks to indoor sports gyms. Indoor sports bouldering gym facilities, first established in Portland in the early 1980's, are today quite numerous and very popular. Today these sports gyms provide quality indoor training and practice environs where dedicated individuals can build their skills base before venturing outdoors to the vast treasure of old and new bouldering sites this micro-region has to offer. This modern trend, mixing gym training sessions with an expansive wealth of new bouldering site options is a far cry from the limited choice of early era bouldering sites like Carver Boulders and BOGB. Indeed, year-round sports gyms have gradually, yet radically increased the appetite for people to step outdoors and

Preston at *Empire Boulders*

explore this fascinating plethora of bouldering opportunities.

Considering the limitations that cold, rainy winter months have on this outdoor activity in western Oregon, it seems a bit odd that the activity has attained considerable increased value. Yet, using each good weather window, and tapping the sunny south-facing (or breezy) aspects of certain sites, you can extend your outdoor bouldering opportunities to virtual year-round sessions. Several mini sites such as Hamilton Boulders and Horsethief Butte offer year-round bouldering.

Portland has not been viewed as a primary bouldering haven in the 90's nor during the early part of this century. Yet with the latest additional string of quality new sites such as Hamilton Boulders, Alpenglow, and the Empire, a quality series of close proximity sites offer superb direct opportunities for today's boulderer who no longer must endure long drives to Sisters Boulders.

So, mix a sweet combination of numerous city-based indoor bouldering gyms, numerous well-established (and new) bouldering sites with 3000+ total problems, stack on top of it Northwest Oregon's largest bouldering site (Lost Lake Boulders), toss into the mix about six months of great bouldering weather, and we may possibly have a nice comprehensive micro bouldering region after all (...maybe). So, grab your rock shoes and chalk bag and hit the road, and go visit some of the wealth found at Portland's best bouldering sites.

This analysis on the activity of bouldering around Northwest Oregon is purely introductory in scope, just one mere edge of the sport, and not a 'complete' discussion of it. Using Lost Lake Boulders as an example: it barely started seeing substantial sending activity in late 2013, yet when it is eventually fully tapped will easily qualify as the biggest bouldering site in this particular micro-region. With all consideration toward all the numerous sites that compose regional bouldering in/near Northwest Oregon, certainly the sport of bouldering has essentially become its own stand-alone sport.

Outdoor recreation based sports in Oregon is increasingly popular, and growing community networks of sport enthusiasts have made shared responsibility stewardship trends integral to their core group message, and have established relational goals in conjunction with local land managers in recent years. Ethical responsibility and an earnest desire to see more openness for climbing or bouldering helps frame citizen communication networks of stewardship based cooperation

CLIMATE

Western Oregon valleys and the snow laden High Cascade Range predominate in douglas fir, spruce and hemlock forests that are often wrapped in misty overcast or drizzly days. The Oregon climate west of the Cascade Range is predominantly wet six months of the year. Pacific marine air weather systems bring an abundance of rainfall that saturates the region, especially from late-October through May. Between the rainy weather patterns when sunshine prevails (May through October) outdoor bouldering recreation ensues in earnest. During this portion of the year mild marine air often mixes with inland Great Basin hot weather to bring a climber-friendly cycle that keeps the region quite comfortable.

During the summer months temperatures average in the seventies to mid-eighties (Fahr-

enheit) with occasional short peaks of blazing hot sunny days reaching the nineties in July and August (infrequently peaking near 100°F+).

On stifling hot days in July and August don't hide because your favorite bouldering site is a boilerplate. Instead go to high altitude stellar bouldering sites that offer ideal 'heat-escape' locales far better than the low elevation bouldering sites (such as Larch Mtn Boulders, Silver Star Mtn on Ed's Trail, Three Corner Rock Boulders, Timberline Boulders, Cooper Spur Boulders, Bulo Point, Lost Lake Boulders, or Rock Creek Boulders). Some folks are determined to crank only V-hard, so full sunshine bouldering may be too limiting on the hottest summer days, but for those who relish VB-V3 there is an unlimited plethora of stuff at all the higher altitude sites, with minimal to zero moss, and a general lack of mosquitoes (at breezy sites).

By late October, the Pacific marine air storm tracks become more active, usually bringing a consistent series of rain showers. The typical winter storm systems generate frequent cold, rainy days with average temperatures in the 35–50°F range. Average annual precipitation in the Willamette Valley near Portland is about 40 inches.

Nearby, in Central Oregon, the world class destination haven of Smith Rock and its surrounding environ offer a infinite variety of virtual year-round climbing and bouldering on welded tuff (at Smith), and an unlimited supply of lowly rimrock basalt formations scattered liberally across the arrid region in a mixed forest of pine and juniper.

In summation: If it is not raining and it's warm – go bouldering; if it's raining go to the eastside of the Cascade Mtn Range to various bouldering sites.

BASIC GEOLOGY

Its a quirk, at least in the eye of a boulderer, that the greatest percentage of large stone clusters found in this region (of high quality and quantity) are composed of andesitic-basaltic rock characteristics. From a geological perspective, this is readily apparent, simply because most of the Pacific Rim volcanoes (from Japan, to the Alaskan archipelago, and from western Canada / western U.S., to the Andes mountain range of South America) actively expelled (in recent history and to this date) voluminous quantities of igneous lava, some of it being old lava flows with andesitic characteristics. Andesite rock, in essence, is water, gas content, bits of sediment, and a healthy dose of silica sprinkled in, all previously subducted by an oceanic plate, conveyor belt fashion down beneath the continental plate. These two plates rub and drag sediment material downward, in a process which heats and melts the rock, pooling into massive molten structures that, being lighter than the surrounding older congealed rock structure, rises slowly to the surface venting explosively as volcanic mountain peaks.

The results of this conjunctive igneous mix produce lighter colored silica-rich lava rock types (breccias, tuffs, andesites, dacites, and rhyolites) of volcanoclastics found along the entire Pacific Rim volcanic string. After long periods of erosional and chemical weathering processes, the resultant forested landscape revealed exposed clusters of large andesitic boulders (or short vertical escarpments), in surprisingly extensive quantities throughout the northern Oregon Cascade Mountain range.

Andesite is compositionally a mineral-rich plagioclause matrix, yielding a natural slightly gritty friction-friendly surface of superb quality, including occasional gaseous vesicle pockets, and parallel joint plains that create edges or ribbing for fingertips and foot holds. Many andesite, rhyolite, and dacite boulders originally congealed as larger bulky structures or bluffs, but were tumbled and survived the initial roll remaining relatively intact in variable sizes 7'-25' diameter (occasionally larger). Variables within the compositional matrix of andesite can be extensive and radical, even if just a short distance lay between two sites (i.e. Alpenglow and Super Heroes). One site may yield minute bits of pyroxene, feldspar, amphibole, biotite or some quartz, while another site will have ⅔ sized crystalline interstices in the plagioclase matrix.

Though andesite is the dominant and preferred bouldering stone in northern Oregon, it's not the only good quality rock available. Larch Mtn Boulders are composed of bullet hard, high-quality peripheral granodiorite, formed from a nearby subsurface batholithic intrusion. Marys Peak near Corvallis has beautiful high-quality gabbro rock, yielding superb friction-friendly bouldering. Near Broughton Bluff, the Magma Zone is basaltic (and slick-*ish*), which may be part of the reason locals tend to avoid this site. At low altitude sites moss and soil may lightly etch the surface of the stone, as well. Another example of smooth basaltic stone is at Horsethief Butte, but the semi-arid environs have given some of the surface aspects a friendly textured patina. Beacon Rock, being an old andesitic volcanic neck of a once very tall mountain, its andesite perimeter lava flows should theoretically still be visible as horizontal slices in the surrounding bedrock terrain, such as the bluff from which the primary string of Cascade Boulders originates.

INHERENT RISKS

Boulderers are like railroad train engineers, wrapped in centric steel-like tendinous muscle, on a sports quest, and sometimes on a sophist quest. The game of bouldering is somewhat like mixing vodka and a race car, so if your not expecting to see a volatile reaction, guess again. Bouldering necessitates logical judgment skills, so consider carefully prior to delving heavily into the outdoor bouldering scene. Beware of the inherent risk of personal injury, especially if you are prodded on with guttural boosts from your bouldering partner. A mixed recipe of this sort sometimes presses beggarly for potentially serious consequences. You might prefer to live without thirteen steel pins holding your ankle together (one of the uglier risks of this sport). When you get high on an 18'-24' tall stone, well above that postage stamp sized crashpad, one mere slip and your 5-day week occupational reality show might end as an internal compression injury, or something far uglier. If your doing a quick send on an 18' hi-ball off the deck, be careful. There is no guarantee that your hands won't peal off first when plowing sideways across an overhung roof. The word 'crash'-pad should provide a clue. Face it, rock climbing is obviously inherently risky, while the bouldering game is a subtle

Larch Mtn Boulders

degree beyond that.

This micro-regions' elusive bouldering sites are broadly distributed, but tend to be densely packed with an average of 20-90 boulder problems per site. The scattered boulder sites (or crags) are usually tree-shrouded, seldom of mega size (like the ultra long TLC crag, or the 1k LLB). Most are just small hidden quaint little pocket gems (by Oregonian standards).

Climbing and bouldering tourism in this micro-region has steadily expanded because various dedicated individuals find solutions to override any non-civilisé muddy quagmire. This bouldering activity has an expanding array of multi-level broad-scoped personalities whose experience and knowledge help to make the activity as valued as it is today.

Sandbag ratings are hopefully at a minimum herein, but you may still encounter some old-school V-grades that will throw you off, yet through diligent site research our team has made lengthy efforts to either know or send many of the boulder problems in this book. In general the ratings aim for consistency on a per zone/area basis only.

Bouldering and rock climbing is an inherently dangerous activity and you could potentially get injured or die from either sport activity. Do not use this book as an instructional manual. Get proper training through a guide service or an educational class with a local outdoor organization. Learn the game gradually tutorially with associates who know how to keep you safe and alive and happy so you can go out bouldering again tomorrow.

Textual and visual errors may exist in this book. You assume responsibility for your own safety, not the book author, nor publisher.

If you have historical beta or development information that is missing from this book, and are inclined to share, or provide feedback, contact us via email with your info. We always aim to improve the accuracy of future book editions.

USING THIS BOOK

BOULDERING GRADE SCALE

Boulder problems use the well-known Verm or V-rating system. This effective grade comparison scale is designed to articulate a relational comparison involving short bursts of energy typical of concise boulder moves, usually three to ten moves long. Though the V system should relate to actual exact lead rock climbing grades it does not quite parallel, due in part to a broad set of variables, which often leads boulderers to an open-ended ratings debate.

The boulder problems in this book are color-coded for ease of identification (on the text and on the photo-diagrams) to fit a general skill level range.

6 INTRODUCTION

In this bouldering book V-scale grading units have meaning. VB means anything 5.9 and below. When the grade is shown as V2 (V4) the left rating is 'standing start' and the parenthesis is a 'sit start' rating. A single grade — like V2ss — is used when the sit start is the common way it's done, thus 'ss' means Sit Start. If no parenthesis grade follows the first grade then the listed grade is generally assumed to be sent as a standing start (which is typical for tall boulders).

Broadly listed ratings (such as V5-7 or V6-V9) are merely an approximation, but it's probably within that range. And that type of graded problem may (or may not) be done. If done (i.e. sent), it's usually narrowed to one single V-grade (but not always) or at the most two (V4/V5) side by side grades.

A question mark '?' after the grade indicates an unknown rating (or possibly not yet seen an ascent). If the grade has a plus '+' symbol it's an open-ended grade assumed to be a minimum of that grade (or stouter); its a mere generic estimate not intended to indicate its final real difficulty. A '/' slash grade means problem is done but not finalized. Any V-number in the guide may, theoretically, be a grade higher or lower than the given rating; it's an inexact science. Lastly, some V-numerics on the topo are mere generic approximations, not implicatory of finality. What is not an exact science is science fiction.

> ## USING THIS BOOK
>
> 1. **Green problems range: VB-V2**
> 2. **Blue problems range: V3-V6**
> 3. **Orange problems range: V7-V10**
> 4. **Red problems range: V11-V17**
>
> This book uses a four-star system to indicate problem quality:
>
> No stars. The problem exists.
> ★ The problem is minor, but interesting.
> ★★ The problem is average quality, but worth doing.
> ★★★ An excellent problem, and it's well worth doing.
> ★★★★ A stellar problem (if you climb at the grade, then definitely do it).

STAR RATINGS

This book uses a simple ★★★★ four-star system. The stars indicate boulder problem quality. The more stars, the better the problem. If no stars, the problem merely exists yet lacks certain appealing qualities.

INFO SYMBOLS

A selection of boulder problem descriptions will have additional icons representative of other challenges found at that particular boulder or problem. These symbols may be listed in addition to the grade and star information.

HI-BALL:

The ⚠ symbol indicates the cutting edge of real high-ball problems at 17' (5-meters) and above. Tall problems below that range may still be spicy, but are not indicated in this guide. This books idea of "hi-ball" is local intent only, and does not relate to hi-ball status elsewhere in the USA.

ROCKY LANDING:

A winters day at *Hamilton Boulders*

INTRODUCTION 7

A jagged edge ⋀ symbol indicates a rocky or hard to protect landing (where extra crashpads and spotters are wise protocol) such as seen in a rocky talus field.

GEAR & SUPPLIES

Quality gear shops exist in both Portland and Vancouver. Each business may stock variable levels of goods needed by today's boulderer. Some common businesses are: **REI** (at several Portland locations), **Next Adventure**, the **Mountain Shop, Oregon Mountain Community, US Outdoor Store,** including online options at these stores (or online at one of your favorite stores).

Popular indoor sports gyms may market a selection of specific gear (chalk, bags, shoes, etc). Indoor sports gyms are great for personal year-round fitness continuity, and are well suited to meet the general climbing public fitness needs especially in this rainy winter western Oregon climate. Some common Portland-Vancouver area indoor sports gyms are: the **Circuit Gym, Clubsport Rock Gym, Movement Gym, Portland Rock Gym, Stoneworks Climbing Gym,** and the **Source Climbing Center.**

Grade Comparison Chart

V Rating	YDS scale
VB	5.9 and under
V0	5.10a/b
V1	5.10c/d
V2	5.11a/b
V3	5.11c/d
V4	5.12-
V5	5.12b/c
V6	5.12+
V7	5.13-
V8	5.13b/c
V9	5.13+
V10	5.14a
V11	5.14b
V12	5.14c
V13	5.14d
V14	5.15a
V15	5.15b
V16	5.15c
V17	5.15d

For those of you who find this select guide booklet to be the perfect tool to a brief selection of the best Gorge Bouldering hotspots, and now you are seeking more places to tap into... you can. To acquire a far more detailed analysis of the entire spectrum of bouldering in this NW Oregon / SW Washington micro-region, you certainly will want to attain the complete analysis of the sport in the ultimate major thesis, the *Portland Bouldering* guide book.

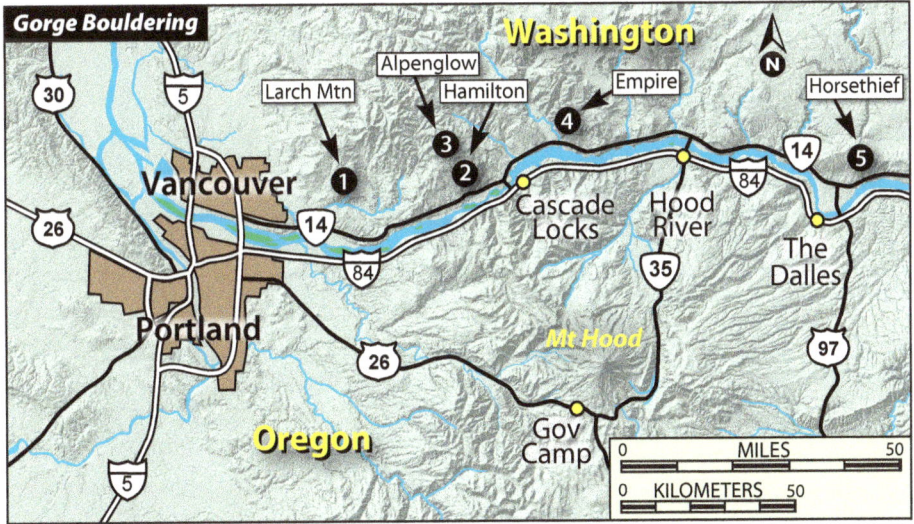

8 INTRODUCTION

When the problem is classic gold only the bold ones get the prize. Sam cranks a classic at the ultra cool Hunchback Boulders.

An Endless World of Bouldering

1

COLUMBIA RIVER GORGE

These extensive bouldering chapters are a detailed treasure of a select set of some of the best bouldering hangouts in the Columbia River Gorge.

The select sites are situated mostly in the western / central part of the Columbia Gorge and though seasonal weather conditions effect each site, due to the south facing aspect of each site you can often utilize most of these havens for 7-12 months of the year. This book covers a specific series of boulder sites (from north of Camas, WA east to Horsethief Butte).

LARCH MTN BOULDERS

High quality granodiorite bouldering on Larch Mountain surpasses all expectations, producing some of the finest bouldering opportunities in our region. Located a mere 23 miles from Portland, this quality site exceeds 100 boulder problems, ranging from VB-V9. Many hi-ball problems (12'-30' tall), stellar rail traverses, overhangs, and techy vertical crimp lines, something for every degree of bouldering. The site is a combination of boulders and rocky outcrops spread over a large area, and in short time certain sections became quite popular, such as the Wild West Bluff formation. The site may eventually yield a minimum of 150+ boulder problems.

The rock has lightly weathered minimally abrasive surficial features that give it a rich texture from long-term weathering processes of the exposed rock surface. The result is ideal for crimps and smearing friction abilities with minimal moss or lichen.

The Larch Mtn rock outcrops are a periferal formation at the utter south end of the Silver Star granodiorite pluton stock.

SEASON

A viable 5½ month fair weather window from mid-May to October is best, with optional days outside of that, as well. Situated at the 3,200' level, with frequent beneficial breezes, cool crisp days in late season (sometimes even in December) with enjoyable bouldering on classic stuff in full sunshine with great scenic views. Spacious views of the entire region looking south over Vancouver and Portland, including northern views of Silver Star Mtn., and east to Mt Hood.

Advantages: no poison oak, no ticks, 2-wheel

Abbott on *Locked & Loaded*, West Fin

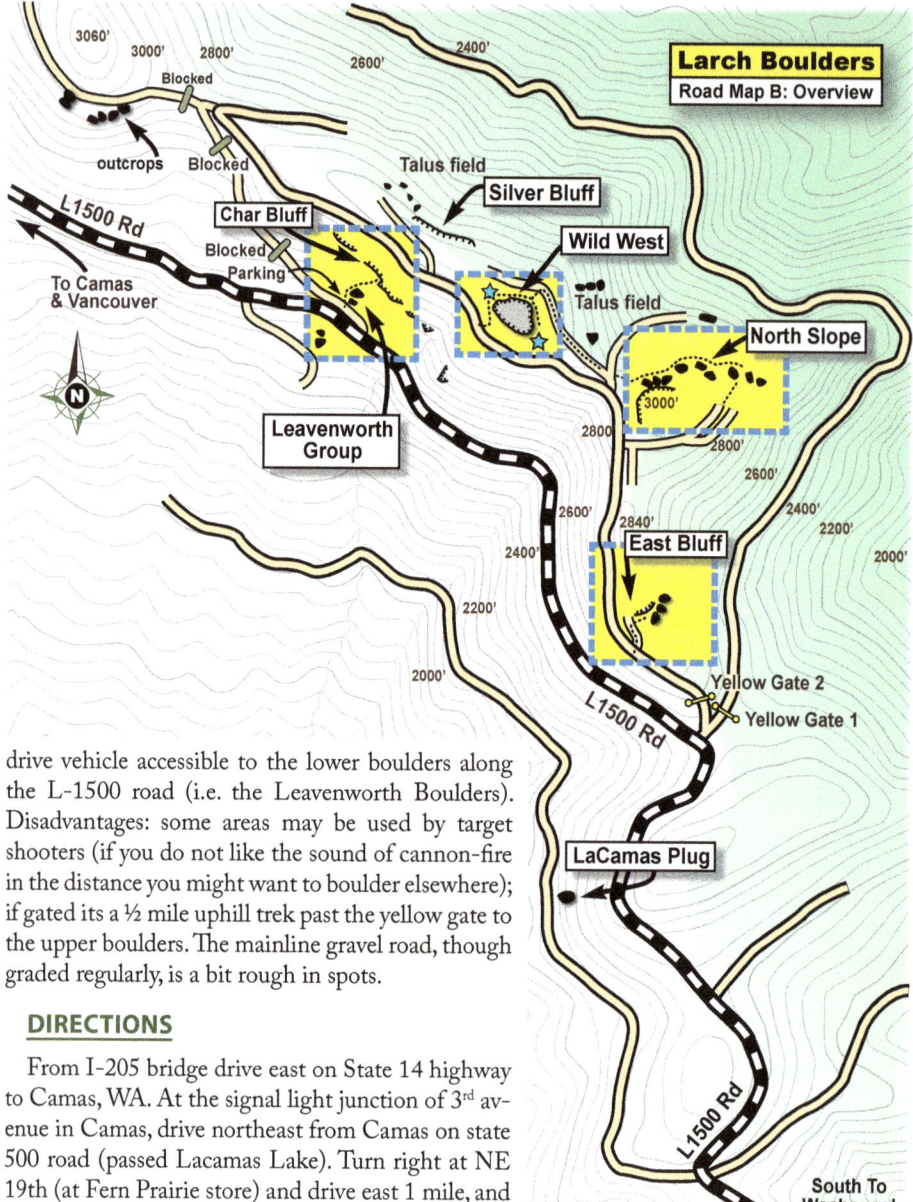

drive vehicle accessible to the lower boulders along the L-1500 road (i.e. the Leavenworth Boulders). Disadvantages: some areas may be used by target shooters (if you do not like the sound of cannon-fire in the distance you might want to boulder elsewhere); if gated its a ½ mile uphill trek past the yellow gate to the upper boulders. The mainline gravel road, though graded regularly, is a bit rough in spots.

DIRECTIONS

From I-205 bridge drive east on State 14 highway to Camas, WA. At the signal light junction of 3rd avenue in Camas, drive northeast from Camas on state 500 road (passed Lacamas Lake). Turn right at NE 19th (at Fern Prairie store) and drive east 1 mile, and take a left at the "Y" and drive north uphill on 272nd. This winds north and east for 2 miles to a 3-way stop intersection. Turn north (left) on 292nd and drive one mile. Turn north onto Livingston Road and continue uphill for one mile till you reach L-1000 forest road which is gravel. Drive on L-1000 for 3-4 miles to a 4-way intersection. Turn right (east) uphill on gravel forest road L-1500 for one mile till it turns right and levels off (passing a yellow DNR gate on the left). Drive east along this generally level portion of the gravel road for one mile to an open area passing another common target shooting spot. Both the Leavenworth Boulder and Black Forest Boulder are located uphill above a secondary road, while the Eiger and Matterhorn stones are below the road.

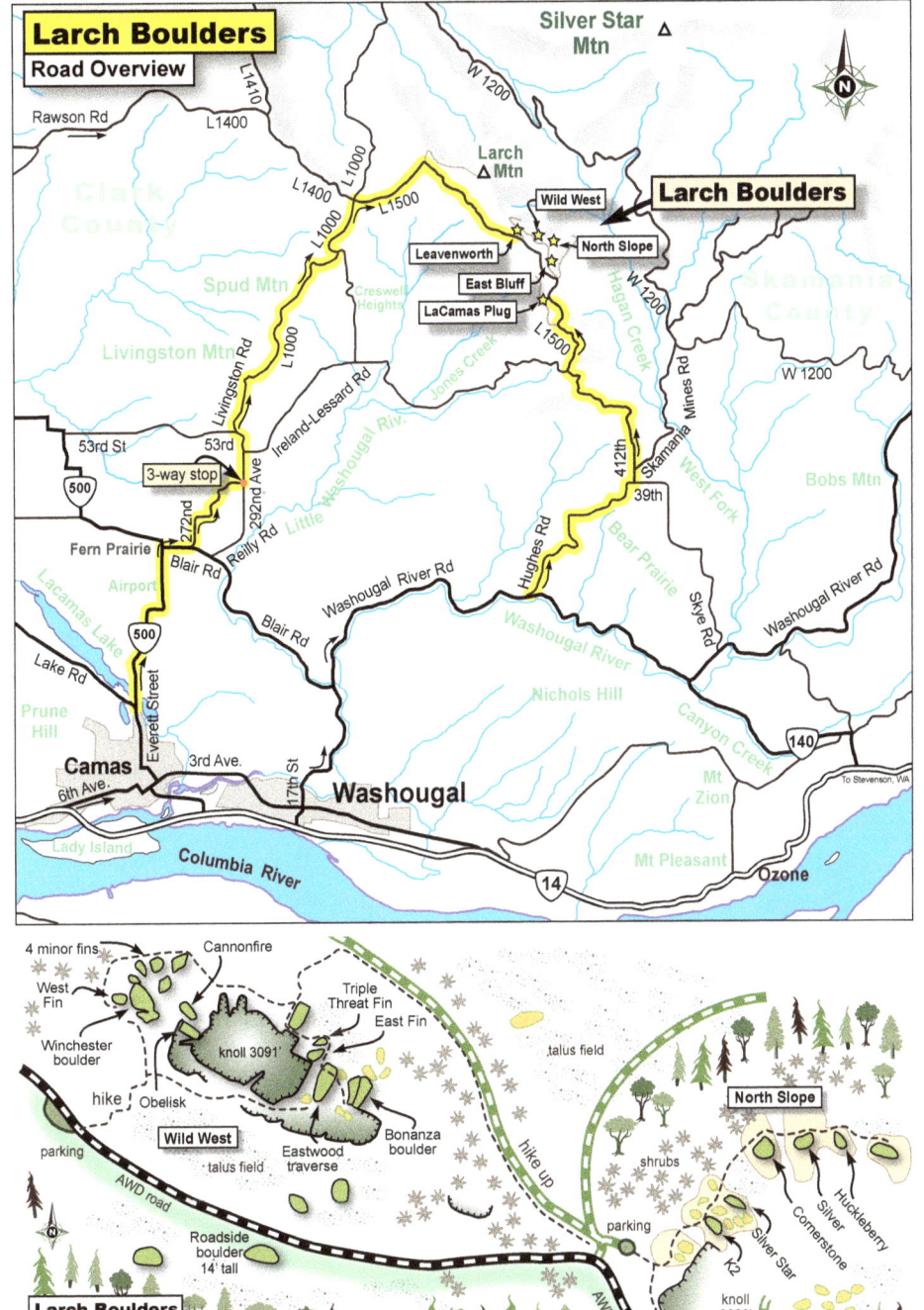

To reach the Wild West Bluff formation at the upper knoll, continue east on L-1500 till you reach a saddle between two hills (at two closed roads with two yellow gates). Park here (near the yellow gate) and hike uphill ½ mile to the bluff. Scramble up the steep rocky slope to either the west side or east side of the butte. Road L-1500 is a bit rough but is 2WD viable.

Note: There are several alternate methods to reach Larch Boulders: via Hockinson, or north from Camas past Fern Prairie store, or up the Washougal River several miles turning left up onto Bear Prairie.

LEAVENWORTH GROUP

The **Leavenworth Boulder** is one of the premier boulders at Larch Mtn., and its situated at the very first locale (when driving north from Camas) on the peak. Park on a dead-end side road directly below the boulders. Walk uphill about 80' to two massive boulders. The Black Forest Stone is the smaller boulder, and Leavenworth Stone is the giant 15' x 30' x 30' behemoth. The flowers are in full bloom in June-July. This is the most convenient bouldering site at Larch Mtn for 2-wheel drive vehicle access. Plenty of powerful overhanging bouldering lines from juggy fun problems to delicate core intensive power crimp-fests.

Leavenworth Boulder

The Leavenworth Boulder is considered to be the rare gem at Larch Mtn., of the type and quality found only once at great bouldering sites. GPS UTM 10t 555669 5061306

Beta is from left to right:

VB Crazy Get Down ★
A short juggy basic problem on west face.

VB (V0) Terminate This ★★★★
Very fun warmup problem on a short hung arête prow.

V1 (V2ss) Super Cool ★★★
Start on the same arête (of previous problem) but on the right side.

V2 (V3ss) Back In The Day ★★★★
Great line with a series of good holds.

V3 (V5ss) Iron Giant ★★★★
The classic center south face line, a 12' tall hi-ball. Start on left pinch, and aim up to a slight groove where better holds near the lip await.

V7 (V8ss) Iron Clad ★★★
Upper body core intensive movement. Start on Iron Giant aim up left, then fall onto the minute rock horn protrusion, then power up to the top near Back In The Day.

V8 Octagon ★★
Quality hard core hi-ball line.

V5 (V6ss) Dragon's Tail ★★★
No jugs route. Start on under clings to thin crimps. Tough to see crimps, and the exit is thin and tricky. A 14' tall hi-ball.

V6 (V6ss) Scorpion King ★★★★
Cool techy hi-ball line with a crucial right hand crimp up high.

VB (V0ss) Embers ★★
On the east face of the block is a series of large steps; sit extends line by starting low on left.

The traverses:

V3 Liquid Metal ★
An uphill rising traverse on the left (west) as-

Leavenworth Boulder • GB 13

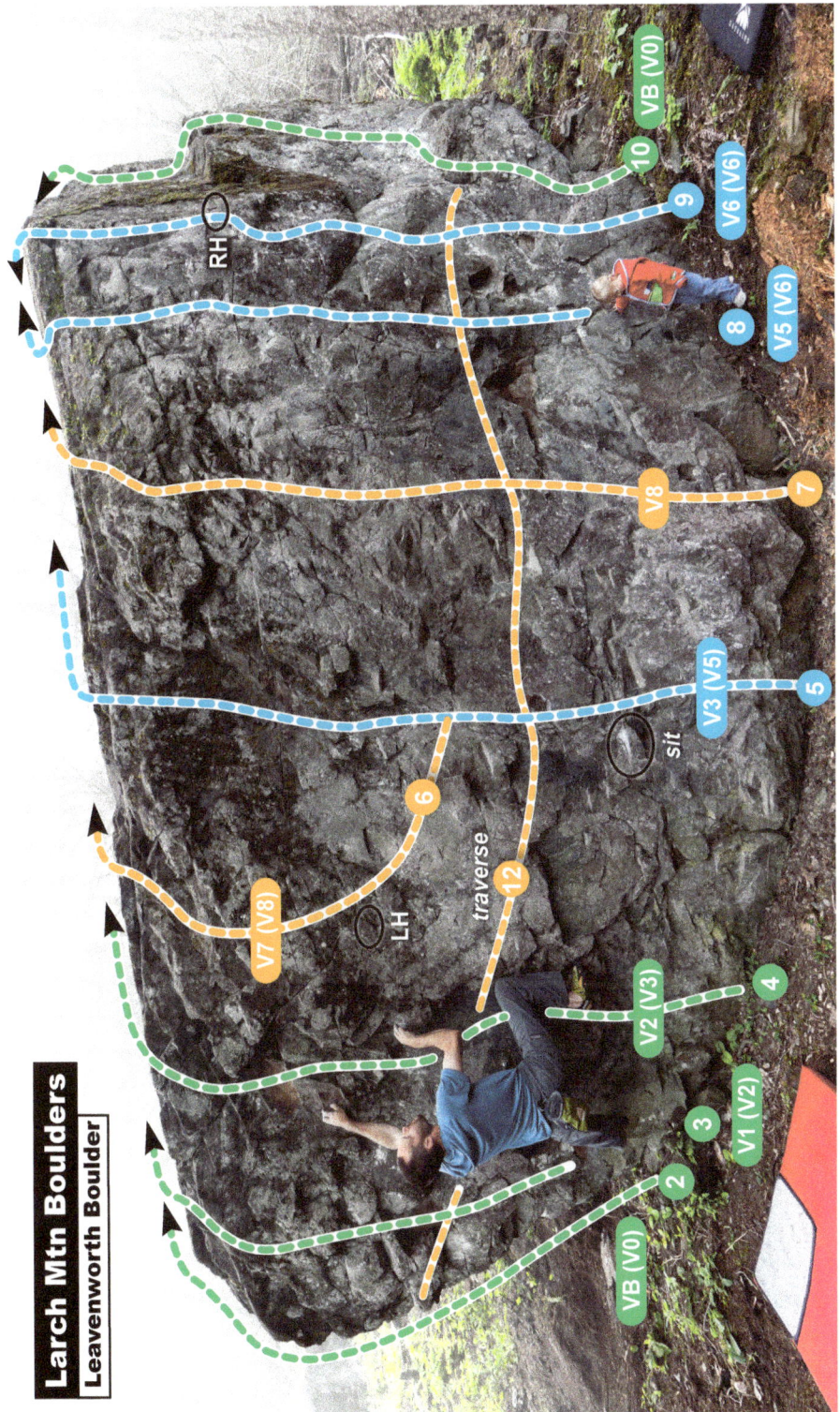

pect of the rock formation.

V9 Leavenworth Traverse ★ ☐
Go from 'Terminate This' to the far rightmost route.

Black Forest Boulder

This boulder is just downhill from the Leavenworth Boulder and offers more quality problems on good rock. Beta left to right:

VB Get Down ☐
A minor down climb on the west end.

V1ss Soot ☐
Just uphill of prow.

V1ss Jungfrau ★ ★ ★ ★ ☐
The overhung classic arête on the west end.

V3ss The Great Escape ★ ★ ☐
Start on next problem and use the sloped face to two small divot holds to exit.

V0 (V0) Climbingruven ★ ★ ☐
Start on small left-facing fins and finish up right on large appearing edges to a not so simple crux exit.

V1 (V3ss) Red Barron ★ ★ ☐
Underclings to good hold and finish same as previous line.

VB (V1) Black Forest ★ ★ ★ ☐
A classic basic line with great holds.

VB Chocolate ☐
Basic fun run.

The Traverse:

V4 Black Forest Traverse ★ ★ ★ ☐
Start on the route #1 and fall into position on the arête, and continue across the south face of the boulder.

Matterhorn Boulder

The Matterhorn and Eiger Boulders are located below the car parking spot at Leavenworth Boulder zone. Use a bulldozer road grade that cuts down from the

Brian on *Junfrau Prow*

Eric on *East Fin*

Matterhorn / Eiger • GB 15

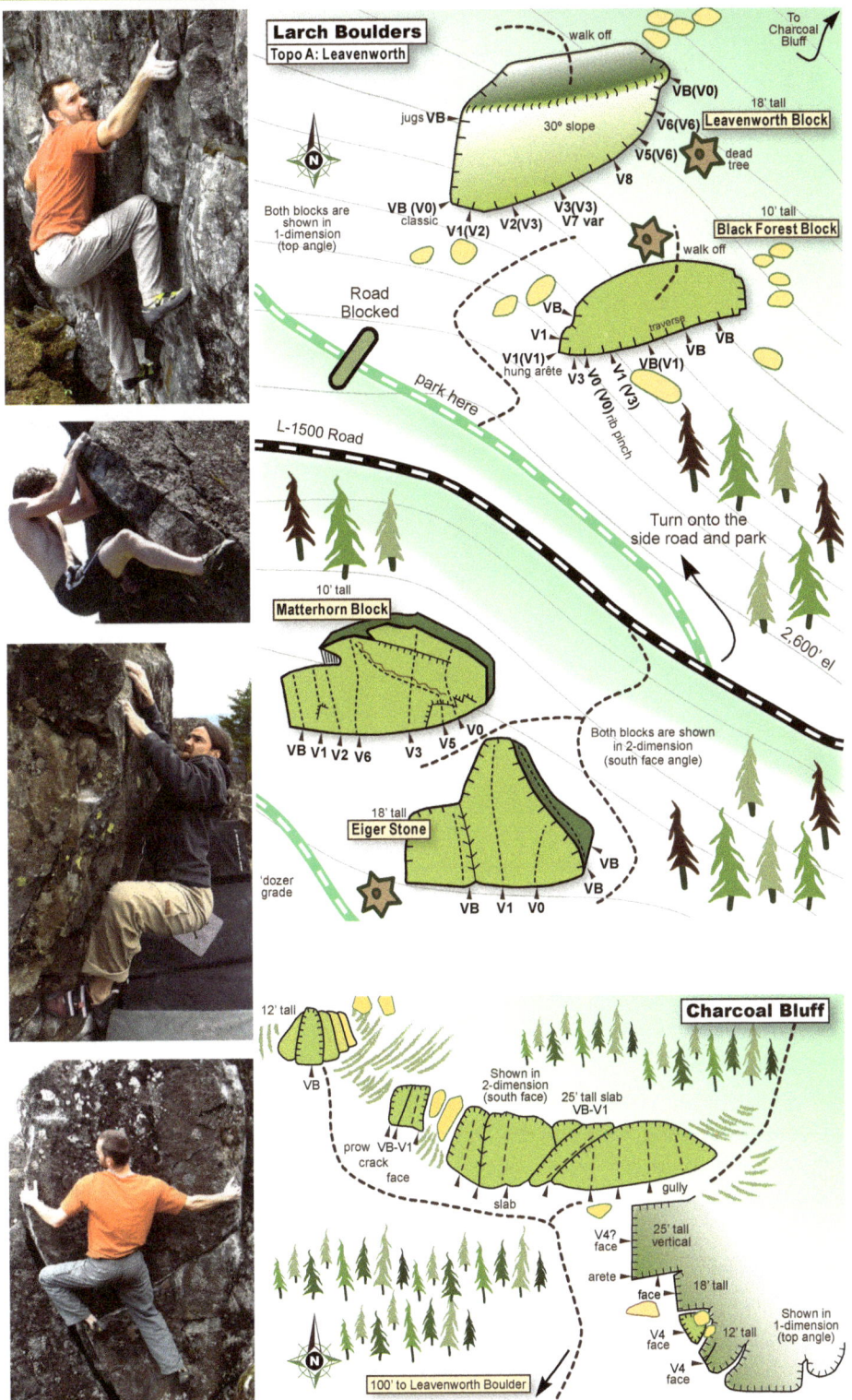

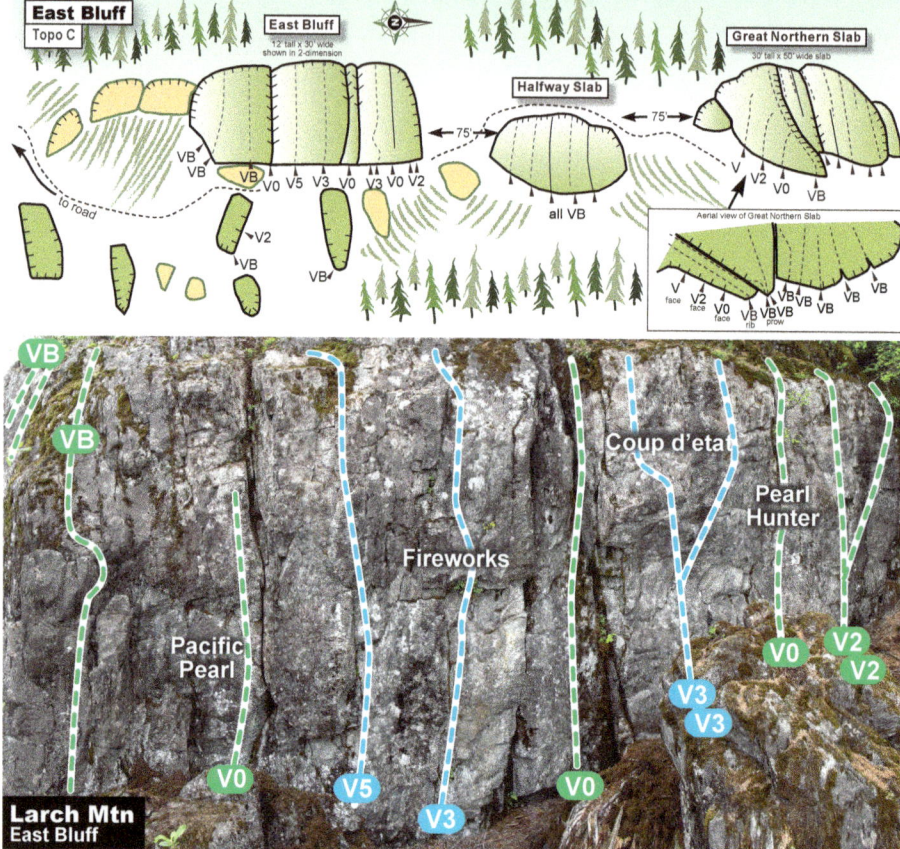

west to the cluster. The Eiger is an 18' hi-ball, and the Matterhorn has a short flat slightly hung face.

VB Hot Butter
The leftmost face line.

V1 Melting Hot ★
Start at the slight undercling.

V2 Sunburn ★★
Move into it from left, then directly up.

V6 Where's da Shade ★★★
The center thin crimps face.

V3 Summertime ★★

V5 Rising Sun ★★★
Start low on right, and run left along the horizontal seam to far left end.

V0 Hot Tin Roof
This is the rightmost crimps problem.

THE TRAVERSE:

V7 Matterhorn Traverse ★★
Traverse entire face, avoid top lip.

Eiger Boulder ⚠

VB Titanic Ego
Leftmost corner.

V1 Whymper's Wonder ★ ⚠
Run the tallest part of the face.

V0 Collateral Damage ★ ⚠
Up south face and exit right onto rib.

VB Rogue Nation
The angled minor rib.

VB Garbage Talk
Short east face slab.

Charcoal Bluff ⚠

Above the Leavenworth Boulder a brief walk (30 yards) uphill is a short cliff forma-

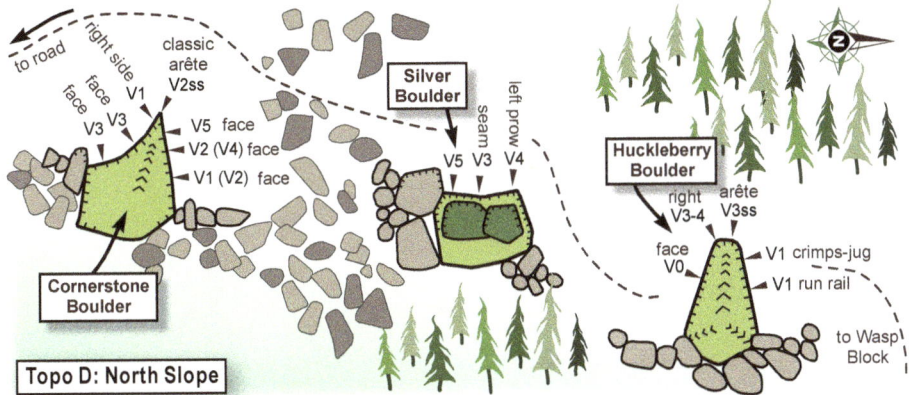

Topo D: North Slope

tion with a slabby 25' wall about 80' wide viable for solo VB-V0 runs. There is a 25' tall hi-ball, 5° overhung flat face with sharp crimp holds (V4?), and several other V4 problems just down to the right at a landing. A minor rocky outcrop (visible from road) 200' east of a tiny stream may offer 4-6 VB problems on a minor 12' face.

East Bluff

A quality east-facing 15' tall by 40' wide bluff (this bluff is visible from the east Yellow Gate). Below the wall 3-4 large boulders yield some minor bouldering. From the first East Bluff walk horizontally to the right in the forest about 70' to reach the Halfway Slab (20' x 30' wide slab with four VB's). About 70' further right is the Great Northern Slab (50' wide x 30' tall, 50° slab) with about a dozen lines. GPS UTM 10t 556439 5060569. Beta is described from left to right.

VB War Zone ☐
Far left crack and left face.

VB House of War ☐
Start off top of small rock pedestal.

V0 Pacific Pearl ★ ★ ★ ⚠
☐
A vertical thin crack.

V5 Count Down ★ ★ ★ ★ ⚠
☐
A thin powerful hung face.

V3 Fireworks ★ ★ ★ ★ ⚠
☐

Techy hung face.

V0 Double Trouble ⚠ ☐
The double crack slot.

V3 Coup d'etat ★ ★ ★ ☐
Hung face (+ 1 variation).

V0 Pearl Hunter ★ ★ ★ ☐
The hung seam.

V1 Frosted ★ ★ ☐

V2 Flakes ★ ★ ☐
The above are two hung face variations.

Two boulders below the east bluff (**VB SOS**, **V2 Loco Citato** (hung jugs), and next **VB Locus Minoris** (lower prow).

Great Northern Slab ⚠ ⛰

V1+ _____ (left face shorty) ☐

V2 Ad Infinitum ★ ☐
Crimps to slopers on face.

V0 Cold Kiss ☐
Short and minor.

VB Slabrageous ★ ★ ☐
A fun slab face near the prow (5.4).

VB Lost World ★ ★ ☐
Start at the point and cruise face and corner up left (5.4). Or climb straight up to top.

VB Hidden Treasure ★ ★
☐
A tall face immediately right of OW.

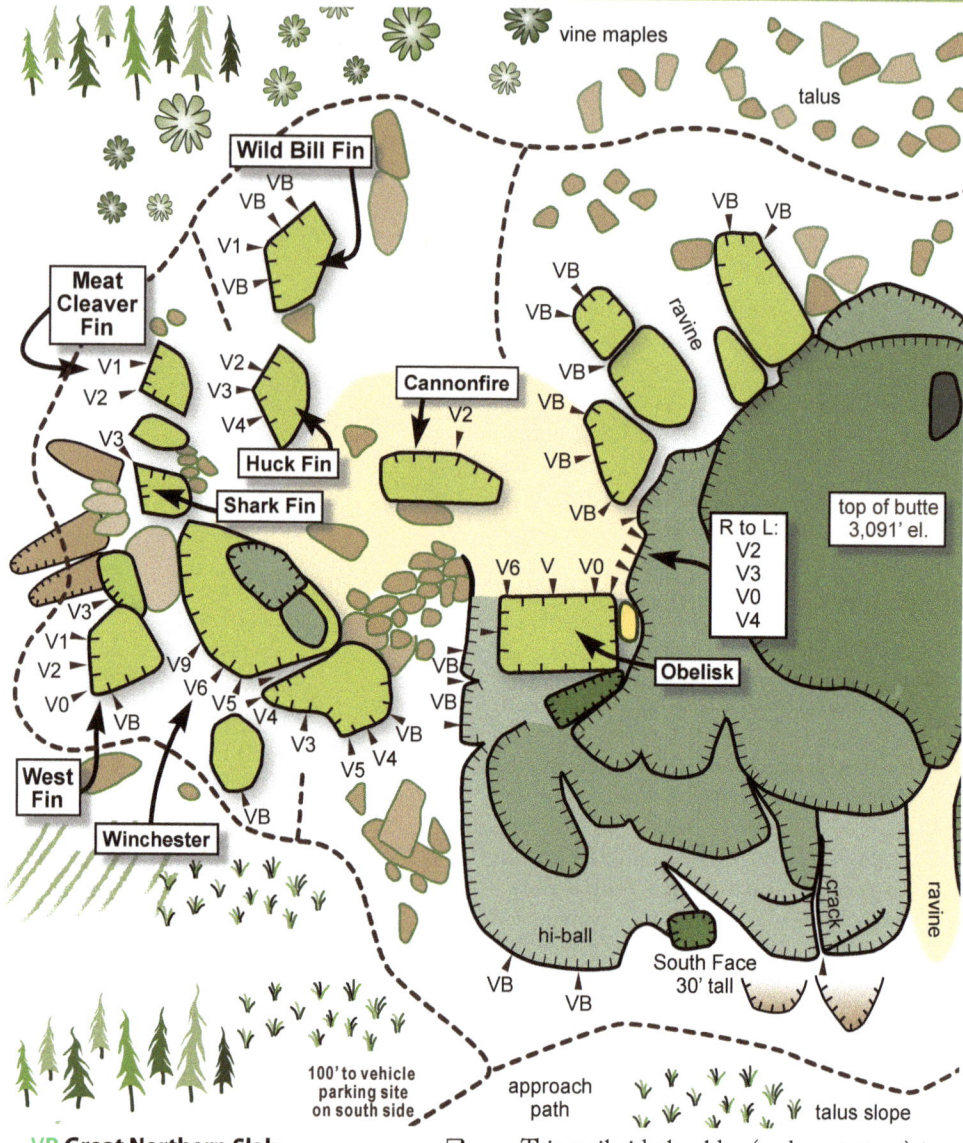

VB Great Northern Slab ☐
A long angled slab.
VB The remainder of the slab is basic.

NORTH SLOPE GROUP

At a flat landing walk east on a narrow trail, then descend north across the base of a talus slope. The site offers a series of five northward sloping talus fields separated by vine maple thickets. A good locale to escape from hot scorching temperatures of summer.

K2 Boulder

This trail side boulder (and next stone) is part of the initial talus slope visible from the road. There are several additional stones in this vicinity to tap. Beta is right to left.

V2ss Locum Tenens ☐
The rightmost line on the stone.

V2ss Locus Standi ☐
Use the sloped nose.

V2ss Lorem Ipsum ★ ☐
Use the large incut jug hold to start then use crimps to finish.

North Slope • GB 19

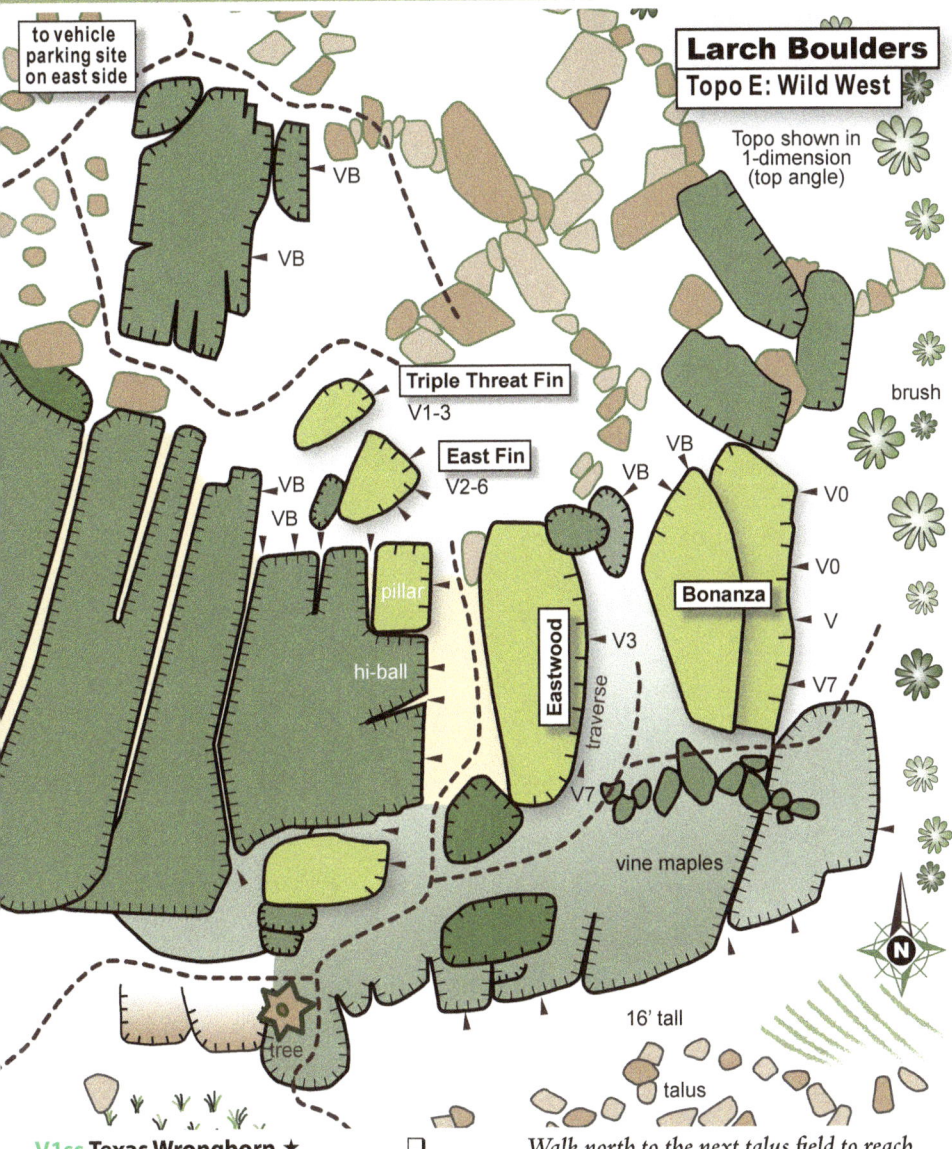

V1ss Texas Wronghorn ★ ☐
Just sit low, grab a high right side pull, high step.

V2ss Lucida Sidera ☐
Leftmost stout line starting on low sloper.

Silver Star boulder

V5 Silver Star ★ ☐
This is slightly uphill of the previous boulder (great views of Silver Star Mtn). The sit start bear hugs both arêtes, finish direct to top.

Walk north to the next talus field to reach the Cornerstone Boulder.

Cornerstone Boulder

A monster sized double-faceted stone with a large roomy crashpad landing zone. The stone is about 14' tall with two main aspects and a prominent 130° overhung arête. Beta is left to right:

V1 (V2ss) Infinite Reality ★★ ☐
Leftmost problem on crimps and slopers.

V2 (V4ss) Cannibals Crowbars Cocktails

★★ ☐

A tech face with crimps. Catch the pinches on finishing rail, move up left and top out.

V5 Modus Operandi ★★ ☐

On the face immediately left of arête.

V1 (V2ss) Land Down Under ★★★★ ☐

Ultra-classic super overhanging arête. The sit start bumps a long reach to a high left hold, then to ample holds on right side.

V1ss Illuminate This ★★★ ☐

Bump up 2-3 times to fat holds at seam, up left to arête, finish to top.

V3 Bad to the Bone ★★ ☐

Corner and face (with variants) busting over small roof on right side.

V5 Cornerstone Traverse ★★ ☐

Full traverse of both facets of the boulder.

Silver Boulder

Overhung north facing aspect offers some wild stuff. Beta is left to right.

V4ss Lone Ranger ★ ☐

Just 'ss' the left prow.

V3ss Hi Ho Silver ★ ☐

Punch past the overhang, then seam, aiming up right.

V5 Silver Bullet ☐

Standing start to dicey mantle.

Huckleberry Boulder

This is a stellar 45° super-overhung rock fin. Beta is left to right:

V1 Bear Treats ☐

Run the rail on the far left shaded side.

V1 Tom Sawyer ★★ ☐

Crimps to a jug, then a tricky mantle onto that large jug.

V3ss Huckleberry Finn ★★★ ☐

Using crimps, angle up onto the left side of the 130° overhanging arête. Difficult to top out.

V4ss Doc Holliday ★★★ ☐

Virtually same as previous except bump up to jug high and right, then up and over the very nose of this 130° feature.

V0 Right Face

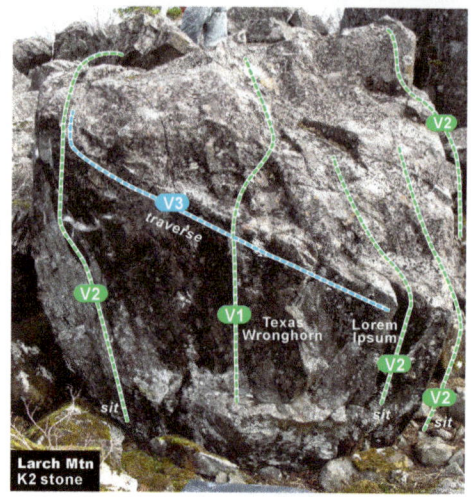
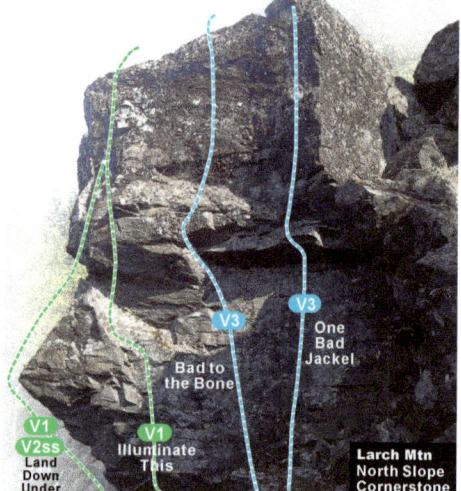

Wild West Bluff • GB 21

the east side of the formation. The west side boulders encompass the four Minor Fins, the mega West Fin, and Bonanza Boulder. Plenty of varied lines and the most common starting place to experience Larch Mtn bouldering.

FOUR MINOR FINS

A group of 4 minor boulders. Most are sit start problems; all well developed.

Wild Bill Fin

This upper left stone offers four minor problems (L to R: **VB**, **V1ss**, **V1ss**, **VB**).

Huck Fin

This upper right stone offers three power-

A minor problem on the right face.

THE TRAVERSE:

V4 Huckleberry Traverse ★★

A very stout traverse of the entire face. Start on the right and swing along on the jugs and positive holds below the nose.

WILD WEST BLUFF

This is a steep sided rock butte great for bouldering, both on the west side and on

ful sit start problems. Beta is is left to right:

V2ss Showdown ★ ☐

V3ss OK Corral ★ ☐

V4ss Most Wanted ★★ ☐

Meat Cleaver Fin

V2ss Meat Cleaver ★★ ☐
The lower left stone. Sit start, reach, cross to jug, find the lip, top out. The thin cleaver blade is long gone.

Shark Fin

The lower right stone is a squat low overhung detached block held in place by stacked blocks (**V3ss Shark Fin**).

West Fin

Its the giant monster 17' tall fin, a very popular fin to warm-up on with ultra cool virtual hi-ball status.

V3 Wrestling with 'Gators ☐
Bust out from the cave on the left.

V1 Gun Runner ★★ ☐
The left edge of the monster fin; odd top out.

V2 Smith & Wesson ★★★ ☐
Send face. V3 rules avoiding large right jug.

VB (VBss) Locked & Loaded ★★★★ ☐
Ultra-classic line. Just sit start low on right by wrapping your hands around the huge lower flake horn on either side, power up, then cross over to the super incut jug on the main fin, and finesse a final move to top out.

VB Pistol ★ ☐
South aspect basic run.

Winchester Boulder ⚠

The ultimate boulder hi-ball rock face at the Wild West knoll that offers a string of impressive powerful problems with enticing and sequential magnificent madness. GPS UTM 10t 556037 5061273.

V9 Mag Seven ★★★★ ⛰ ☐
The ultimate power line at the knoll. Start at the crack, and power up left along the 25' long rising left leaning classic 20° overhanging prow. The ultra thin crux is at mid-point with

a long reach to latch a flat jug, then continue on positive holds up leftward till you top out on the block. **Magnum** is a variation exit.

V0 (V6ss) Winchester ★★★★ ⚠ ☐
This is a 25' tall crack with slightly overhung

Abbott on *Winchester Boulder*

Winchester / Obelisk • GB 23

Larch Mtn
Winchester Stone

standing start opening moves, then solid easy crack with jugs and steps on the upper half. The full Winchester sit starts under the 65° overhanging jam crack (V6ss), crank out with finger and foot jams, then up the entire route. FA onsite Mr O, the full sit by Mr A. The Slayton eliminate is V7 (**Pistol Whipped**); start on **Mag7** and join higher in the **Winchester** crack.

V5 Breach Loader ★★ ⚠
Just right of Winchester. Face crimp start then merges up left into Winchester.

V0 Gutter Ball ⚠
The deep chimney.

V4ss Born on the 5th of July ★★★★
A superb line that begins 'ss' under an arête, power up the arête to finish on easy terrain. Immediately right of the deep chimney.

V3 Girls with Guns ★★ ⚠
Slightly hung scoop with tricky hi-ball move to top out.

V5 (Run For Cover?) ★★ ⚠
Thin techy face starts on bulge nose just right of a scoop; finish on steep slab.

V4 Surrender
Crimps along a seam on steep face.

VB ____
Low angle slab.

Cannonfire Boulder

V2ss Cannonfire ★
A large oblong boulder just downhill in front of the Obelisk Stone. Low angled traverse problem. V4ss ultra low direct.

The Obelisk (aka Shoebox)

At the rim-top overlooking the West Cluster is a stunning four-sided stelae or stele shaped block perched on the edge on a 15' vertical drop. It is a stunning powerful looking block with bouldering on the north aspect. Beta is from left to right.

V0 Left Face

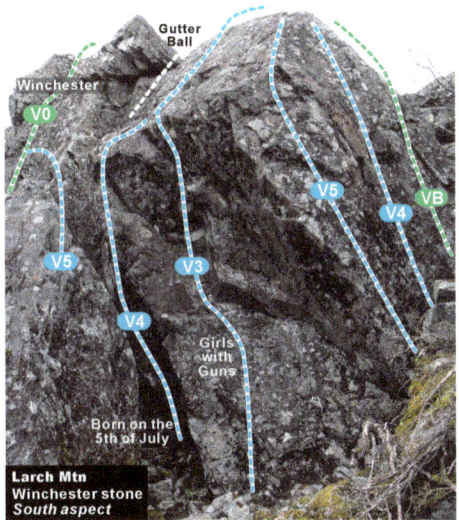

Larch Mtn
Winchester stone
South aspect

Minor face on far left.

V0 Pharoah ★ ☐
The north side jam crack.

V_ (?) _____ ☐
North face thin crimps face potential.

V6 Fortes Fortuna Adjuvat ★★ ☐
The exposed vertical hiball northwest arête.

Directly below the Obelisk on the west side is a short 11' tall bluff with 4 minor problems (range VB-V0) and a short jam crack.

Rimtop Face

Immediately uphill (east) of Obelisk is a short 12' tall bluff. Beta from right to left as if departing from the Obelisk.

V2 _____ ★ ☐
The thin crimps face (rightmost).

V3 Right to Remain Silent ★★ ☐
The left thin crimp face.

V0 Crack ★ ☐
The basic corner crack.

V4ss Meatish Sweetballs ☐

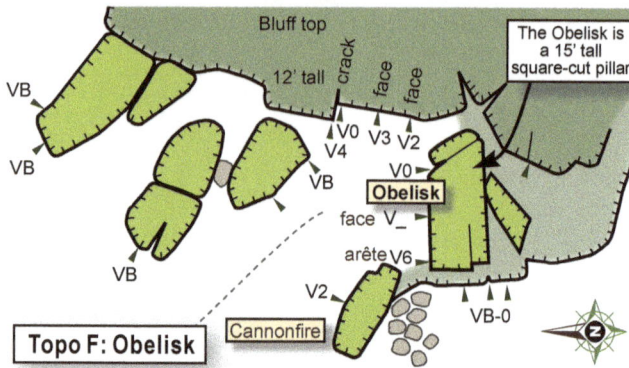

Topo F: Obelisk

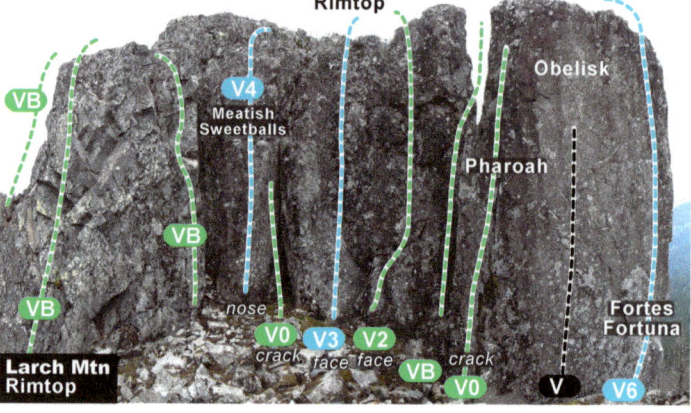

Prow immediately left of crack cleft.
Several more problems exist as the bluff trends downhill northward (about VB-V0).

EAST SIDE (OF WILD WEST BLUFF)

An extensive group of boulders, outcrops, and fins located on the east side of the Wild West butte formation.

East Fin

The exhilerating East Fin has three cool problems. This is a radically overhung 45° slice of rock. The obvious east side fin.

V6ss East Fin ★★★ ☐
Sit start low on undercling, then mid-crimp, and long reach for lip.

V3 Straight Out Of Camas ★★ ☐
Start mid-face on face holds, then catch the lip out right.

V2 Mobile Chunks of Liquid Carbon ★★ ☐

East Side of Wild West • GB 25

Larch Mtn
East Fin

The whole rail starting low on the right and run entire lip to far left.

Triple Threat Fin

Just to the right of East Fin is this overhanging cool tall fin with jugs on the entire upper part.

V1 (V3ss) Triple Threat ★★★★ ☐
Standing start uses the uppermost undercling. The triple undercling sit start (V3ss) begins on a crack undercling on left outside and an inside right undercling, then go up to the second and third undercling onward to the top.

The rocky rimtop formation behind the two primary fins offer five VB faces, corners, or offwidths (all done). The bluff gets hi-ball (left of East Fin) and is generally avoided.

Eastwood Boulder

This is the reason to be at Larch Mtn.

V7ss Eastwood Traverse ★★★★ ☐
A flat laying 25' long thin block of rock with a stellar hand-foot rail traverse. This is the premier attraction. The rail is an upside-down wrestling match, a horizontal traversing physical enduro power line 4' off the ground.

V4ss Eastwood Direct ★★ ☐
Starts on a hollow flake and goes out the center overhang as a mantle.

Abbott on *Winchester*

On *Shooting Gallery*, Bonanza Boulder

Sam on *Magnificent Seven*

Bonanza Boulder

A few yards downhill from Eastwood Boulder is the Bonanza Boulder, a 17' hi-ball with 3 problems on a cool vertical rock face. Beta is L to R:

V7 Shooting Gallery ★ ★ ★ ★
rides the left arête and crescent moon undercling as high as you can (a right hand-heel match will help), then small face crimps and foot smears.

V8+ (?) ⚠
A difficult center line (project).

V0 Jewel Heist
This is a long reach from a jug to a jug, mantle to a stance, then corner to top.

North Face Bluff ⚠

From the Wild West Bluff formation walk north to a rutted track and follow this west to reach a north facing wall 15' tall by 45' long which may offer some steep bouldering.

Roadside Boulder ⚠

One large 17' tall roadside block just under the access gravel road near a parking spot on the south side of the Wild West knoll. Beta is left to right: V0 West Slab, V1 Slab Center, V1 Spooky Slab, V1 Broken Arrow (east face), V0 NE face. Nothing special; just tall.

Bulls Eye Boulder Cluster

This is a cluster of blocks just below the upper road, but in a near direct line from the lower target shooting site. Located on the last ridge before the upper road ends at a flat landing where the road cuts back hard to the north side. A closed 'dozer grade descends downhill to the Leavenworth Boulder site. Mr Davis sent the obvious horn (ala nearby shooters) at V0-V1.

The area on the first and second knoll have a number of other outcrops and boulders, most necessitate considerable walking and

are likely not to see much bouldering activity.

LaCamas Plug area

The area at the LaCamas Plug has minimal bouldering options nearby. Drive to Jones Creek Motocross parking area, then continue on L-1610 gravel road uphill to junction of L-1510 road. Go left (uphill) on L-1500 for ¾ mile, then take a left onto an unmarked graveled road, and follow this downhill for ¾ mile. Walk about 2 minutes uphill from the road to the rock plug. A minor selection of boulders exist on either side of the outcrop.

Eastwood Traverse

A Stellar Year-Round Haven

2

HAMILTON BOULDERS

Crankin' a V4 on Whrisky Boulder

Stellar compact arena of boulders in the midst of a complex south-facing talus field in a state park environment. The visible qualities being ideal, the Hamilton Boulders (aka Horse Camp) has become one of Portland's hotspot gems. And for good reason—it fits a trident combination difficult to match (low elevation, sunny locale, minimal moss), virtual year-round accessibility (except perhaps in July-Aug), and a powerful string of superb quality lines ranging from VB to V11. High quality andesite stone with ideal friction-ability, the site has appeal for its tightly packed core of large sized stones with considerable overhung aspects to swing like a chimp on. Andesite surficial texture of impeccable quality, retains a fine soft grit phenocryst matrix that offers superior grip and smear ops, allowing lines to be realistic regardless of its steepness.

The lower core cluster is a mere 2-minute walk from the parking lot to the first big boulder. A decent path leads into the heart of an amphitheater, a closely packed cluster of huge stones (11'-18' tall). The entire boulder field is extensive, but does offer additional gems as isolated blocks, or small clusters (on difficult to negotiate terrain where diligence and agility are crucial). There are three main clusters (to date), but the entire talus field has been researched and some distant objectives are being tapped. The talus field is an open slope (with minor brush and substantial poison oak) so a savvy individual can generally navigate to the second and third tier clusters easily. A 1-2 crashpad minimum recommendation site. The perfect place to be to catch a send in the middle of a long cold winter season.

DIRECTIONS

Drive east on State Route 14 from Vancouver, Washington for 35 miles to Beacon Rock State Park. Turn left (north at the Ranger Office) on paved Kueffler Road, drive uphill 1 mile, turn right onto a gravel road and continue ¼ mile on this to the Horse Camp parking lot and hiking trail. This is an upper extension of the state park that is commonly used by both hikers and equestrians. Walk north past the white gate for 200', then follow a track left to the obvious talus field, following a cairn coordinated path to the core amphitheater. Extra pointers: good cell phone reception; it is a state park tourist fee required site.

28 HAMILTON BOULDERS

LOWER TALUS FIELD

The lower talus field is the primary bouldering zone where most people go initially. It's short walk from the parking spot make it the ideal destination hangout. This zone is highly developed and offers an extensive selection ranging from easy to ultra power lines.

Boulder 1 (Sunspot)

The first boulder you will see as you step up onto the talus field, shining boldly, and beckoning.

V1 Freaky Flake ★★
Climb a rail on the left portion of this tall face.

V7ss (?) _____ ★
Low and thin crimps on the right face.

The next three minor boulders are located just below the path, and are easy to miss en route to the popular core group.

Boulder 2 (below path)

V4ss _____

Low start on left (launch).

V6ss _____
A low problem on the right (run a rail).

Boulder 3 (Giggles)

V0ss _____
A minor line starting on the right.

V0ss _____
Minor starting on the left.

Boulder 4 (below path)

V3 Right Face
Send just the outer nose.

V2 Left Face
Power up just left of outer point on a sloper rail.

Boulder 5 (Yayo)

A poplar boulder located just below the path. The lower left aspect yields some brief powerful problems. Beta is left to right:

V7ss Direct ★
The leftmost direct on the downhill aspect.

V6ss Chopin ★★★
The lower left aspect using a slippery rail.

V3ss Prow ★★
Use prow, but stay on left side (right hand use prow) and angle left to top.

V2ss Prow Exit Right ★

Hamilton Boulders • GB 29

Generally same as above, but exit right to top.

V1 Slab Left ★ ☐
The slab at center of the block (east aspect).

V2 Slab Right ☐
The slab on the upper rightmost part of block.

THE TRAVERSE

V5 _____ ★★ ☐
Traverse the entire block (both aspects).

Boulder 6 (Elephant)

Located just below the path, but has a large south-facing aspect. Beta is right to left:

V2ss _____ ★ ☐
The rightmost problem next to the talus.

V2ss Elephant ★ ☐
Send the right prow (VB stand).

V1ss Elephant Ear ★ ☐
The center slab (south side).

V1ss _____ ★ ☐
Climb the left prow.

VB _____ ☐
The west aspect of the stone.

Boulder 7 (Shorty)

V0ss Left Shorty ★★ ☐
Left super shorty.

V2ss Shorty ★ ☐
Center-right shorty.

Boulder 8 (Cave)

V2ss Short Pillar ★ ☐
The flat face of minor block just right of cave.

V7ss Cave ★ ☐
Punch out the low cave.

V1ss _____ ☐
The left side of cave.

V2ss Lip Traverse ☐
Traverse the lip of the cave.

Boulder 9 (Mcnugget)

It's short but right alongside the path so its

Coordinates for the core amphitheater at Hamilton Boulders:
GPS UTM 10t 575298 5054834

30 HAMILTON BOULDERS

Hamilton Boulders

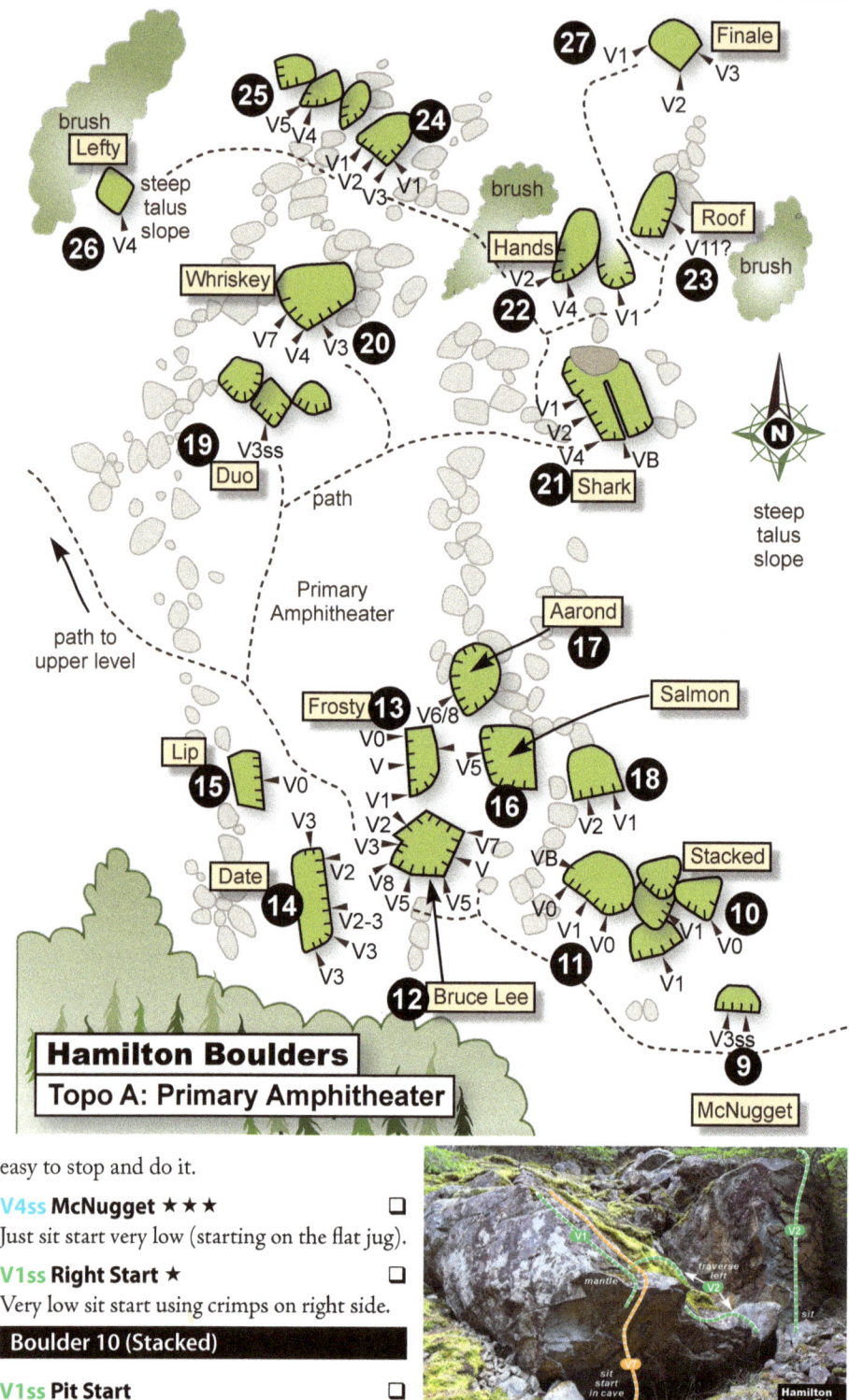

Hamilton Boulders
Topo A: Primary Amphitheater

easy to stop and do it.

V4ss McNugget ★★★ ☐
Just sit start very low (starting on the flat jug).

V1ss Right Start ★ ☐
Very low sit start using crimps on right side.

Boulder 10 (Stacked)

V1ss Pit Start ☐

Hamilton Boulders • GB 31

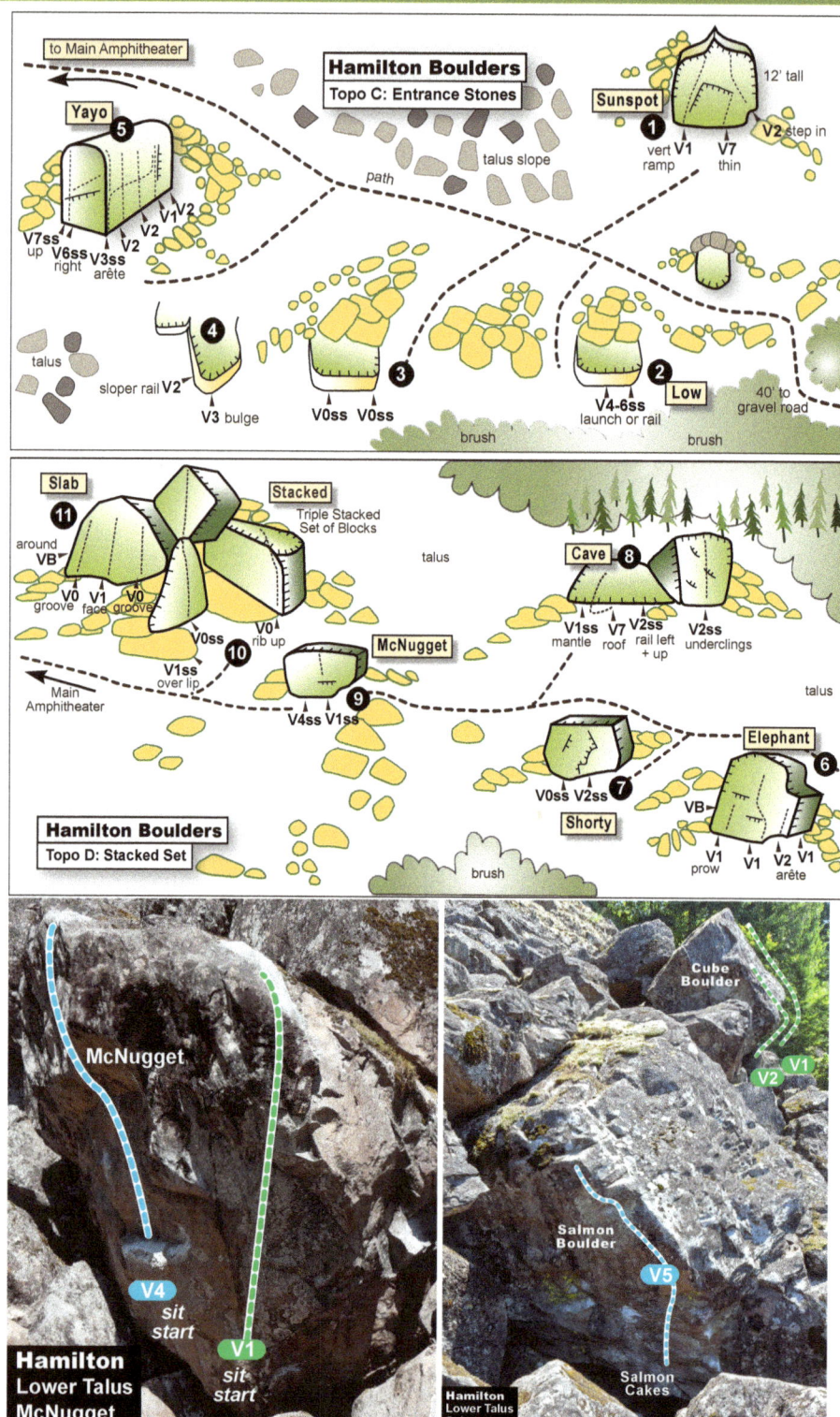

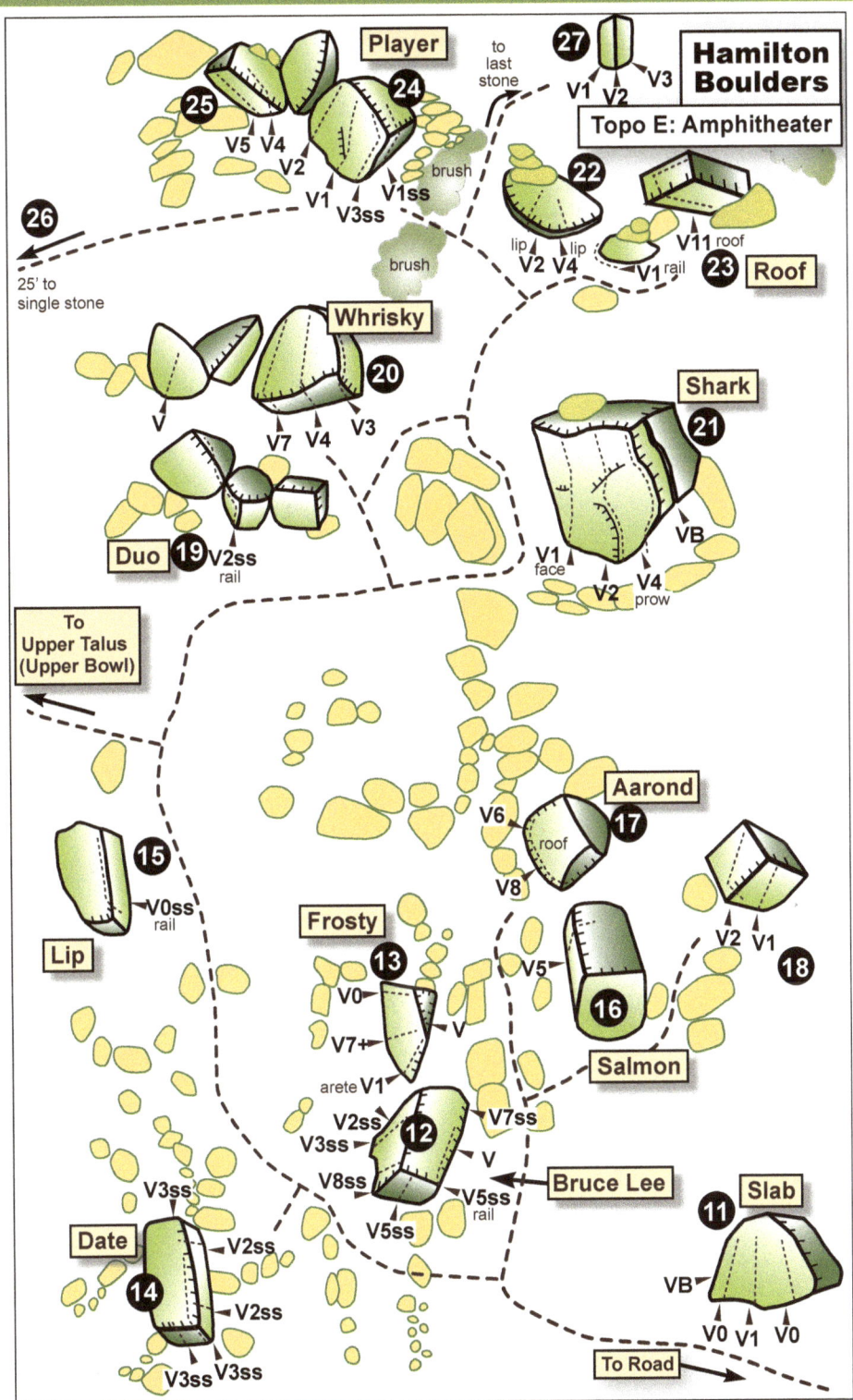

Climb out of a tiny pit up a shorty face.

V0 Stacker ★ ☐
Climb up the entire double stack of blocks.

V0 Rib Rail ★ ☐
A minor rib rail on the right-most block.

Boulder 11 (Big slab)

V0 Left Slab ★ ☐
Send the left part of the long angled slab.

V1 Center ★ ☐
Send the center of the slab.

V0 Right Slab ☐
Climb the right part of the slab.

Boulder 12 (Bruce Lee)

Certainly the reason to be here, because this boulder is a classic. The stone is tucked in a slight low spot, and though the lines may seem short most are quite unique problems.

V7ss East Arête ★★★ ☐
Sit low and power the well hung east arête.

V_ss (?) _____ ☐
Center crimps on the well hung east aspect (project).

V5ss Enter the Dragon ★★★ ☐
Traverse left to right along the entire east lip (to East Arête).

V5ss _____ ★★★ ☐
Sit start low using crimps on the south side only.

V8ss Fluid Like Water ★★★★ ☐
Power up left side, then transition to right side of the hung arête, then pull over lip. Classic!

V3ss Kato ★★ ☐
Brief face moves on overhung large holds (located on west aspect).

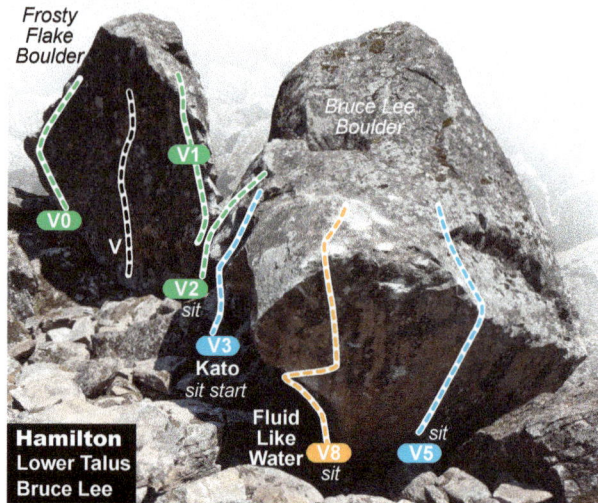

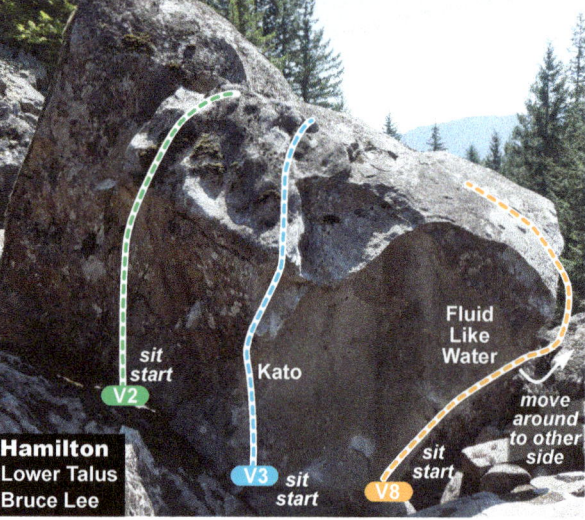

V2ss Johnny Law ★★ ☐
The far NW aspect yields one more.

Boulder 13 (Frosty Flake)

This is a tall thin flake immediately next to the Bruce Lee boulder.

V1ss Frosty Flake ★★ ☐
South prow of the flake starting low.

V0 _____ ★ ☐
Start on north prow and cruise as up-over traverse of entire flake.

V_ss (?) _____ ☐
Possibly in middle west face.

Boulder 14 (Date)

A squat thing just to the west of Bruce Lee boulder. Beta is right to left:

V3ss _____ ★

Sit start very low at the uttermost north side in a nook using crimps.

V2ss Cheap Date ★★

Sit start very low and crimp up from a nook on main east aspect.

V2ss Variations ★★

Several low variants on the same east aspect.

V3ss Left End

Lower leftmost hung point, crimp up over.

V3ss Traverse All ★★

Begin on the leftmost downhill aspect, move up onto lip, then hand traverse the lip rightward.

Boulder 15 (Lip)

V0 Lip Traverse

Minor traverse left to right along lip.

Boulder 16 (Salmon Cakes)

Superb quality boulder problem that's well worth doing.

V5 Salmon Cakes ★★★★

Begin very low in minor pit on a slightly overhung aspect using a series of round hand edges. Several variants exist. A classic.

Boulder 17 (Aarond)

The epitome of roof-ishness is what makes the problems on this boulder appealing.

V6ss A-Aron ★★★★

Crawl into the far back side beneath this flake boulder. Begin on the back inner side of the overhang, foot force, grasp horizontal, reach outer lip and mantle it.

V8/9ss Aarond the World ★★★

Same start as previous, but power along the entire lip, then mantle over at far south end.

HAMILTON BOULDERS

V7ss _____
Traverse just the lip.

Boulder 18 (Square)

V2 _____
Send face on the left.

V1 _____
Send problem on the right.

Boulder 19 (Duo)

V2ss _____ ★
Begin on a round incut rail on the lower block, transition up left onto the second block.

Boulder 20 (Whrisky)

Another powerful reason to be at the Hamilton Boulders. This tall block has a substantial overhanging south aspect that juts out initially making the opening moves dedicated and heady like ~~beer~~ whiskey. Beta is left to right:

V7 Whrisky Left ★
Punch out the left side big undercut, then up vertical face above.

V4 Whiskey Business ★★★
Punch out the center from the undercut base, then up the center of the face on crimps.

V3ss Water to Whiskey ★★★
Sit start low on the rightmost side. Punch out and over the lip then up easy terrain.

Boulder X (minor #1)

V_ (?) _____
Located on a minor block 20' west of Whrisky.

Boulder 21 (Shark Tank)

This is a very popular 12' tall vertical face. Beta is left to right:

V1 Left Face ★★
Cruise the left face of a tall face (west aspect).

V2 Center Face ★★★
Cruise the center of tall face. The problem splits at mid-height and can go either R/L to exit.

V4 Right Face ★★★★
Cruise up the right tall face (at the prow).

VB Right Crack
A fat crack on the right south-facing aspect.

Boulder 22 (Her Shirt)

V2ss Bad Touch ★
Brief thing on left side as a heel hook.

V4ss Her Shirt ★★
Brief thing under it going to the right via all incut jugs.

Boulder X (minor #2)

V1ss _____
Located on a minor block to the right of previous boulder.

Boulder 23 (Her Skirt Roof)

V11 (?) Her Skirt
Toe hooks and long reaches under the roof to the lip then over it. Project? Roof Boulder.

Boulder 24 (Player)

Beta is from left to right:

V2ss Chocolate Thunder ★
The utter leftmost side of block on a round bulge using crimps.

V1ss Center ★★
The center face using the crimps only.

V5ss Vanilla ★★
The right rounded arête. Grade is V5 if cruising leftward along face (easier if straight up).

V1ss Tug Job ★★
A one move run, starting hung going to jugs.

Boulder 25 (Hands Down)

V5ss Her Pants ★
Start low, power the left underside, right hand along lip to finish, then over.

V4ss Her Shorts ★
Start low on right underside, then up right.

Boulder 26 (Lefty)

V4 _____
Located about 20' west of the previous boulder group. A short crimps face problem.

Boulder 27 (Finale)

This stone is located just above the Her Skirt Roof Boulder. Nice problems. Beta is described left to right:

V1 _____ ★
Send the left rounded nose.

V2 _____ ★★
Climb the center face on crimps.

V3 _____ ★★

Send the right arête on crimps.

Boulder 28 (Tumbler Lower)

This stone (and the next) is located high above the gravel road where the path initial branches off. Take the foot path to the lower talus, then bust directly uphill rightward on steep talus till it eases near this minor group.

VB-V0 ☐

All options (5 each) are very basic.

Boulder 29 (Tumbler Upper)

The Upper Tumbler stone is this south facing block. Beta is left to right:

VB, V0, VB ☐

UPPER TALUS FIELD

See the *Portland Bouldering* book for specific details about the approach hike up to this upper zone. The illustration maps in that book provide details on the existing tapped product. One of the superb gems in the upper field you may want to visit is Slashface Boulder. There is some potential yet to be tapped in the upper zone, some of it scattered a fair distance in various clusters. There are scattered thickets of poison oak brush to venture through just to reach the Midway Cluster and the Upper Talus Field, and that alone is enough of a detraction to keep some visitors at bay. Bouldering at the Lower Talus Field has enough quality problems suitable for most people.

Slash Face Boulder

This is one of the classic boulders in the Upper Talus Field. Though a long hike (and some poison oak to negotiate) its well worth the grunt gettin' there just to send it.

V4ss Slash & Burn ★ ★ ★ ☐

The ultra cool hung prow. Sit start low using crimps on both sides of prow, and top out.

V7ss Slashface ★ ★ ★ ☐

The ultra stellar west aspect using a series a very thin slanted crimps.

Gem Quality Bouldering Haven

3

ALPENGLOW BOULDERS

Certainly noted for being one of Portland's finest bouldering areas, Alpenglow holds a concentrated spectrum of VB-V10 problems situated on an open south-facing talus slope, surrounded by a fir forest with impeccable scenery, superb quality bouldering on stones ranging in size from 9'-18' tall, with the fattest stone measuring at nearly 35' in diameter. Alpenglow is a high-altitude locale overlooking the Columbia Gorge. The weather-scoured dacite rock is ideal for 'chalk-and-send' bouldering (about 50 problems and several traverses). The rock surface texture is composed of a slight fine grain quality (no moss), natural divots, edges and smears, rippled textured surficial features, steep vertical faces (both thin techy and jug lines), overhung aspects, dicey hi-ball lines, VB fun runs, and prows. All the quality you could ask for merged into a single core site offering a fine back-to-back list of classic boulder problems found in this region. This is a 1-2 crashpad recommended site.

HISTORY

This site was specifically tapped by Mr Abbott and two close associates (Dave and Shane) starting way back in early 2002 (the team did 85% of all problems). As they returned late one October day from 3-Corner Rock bouldering they spied the Alpenglow cluster just above the tips of the trees. They parked along the roadside and walked up to the untapped site and were very impressed. But alas, the next day fall season rains began in earnest and neither were able to conquer the place until spring 2002. The site was aptly named Alpenglow Boulders by Abbott after seeing quality late in the day sunset hues. A few very stout problems were tagged in about 2014 by several locals and a few more in 2018 by Sam. Today, only a few random lines remain untapped on Shark and Hood Boulder.

SEASONS

Weather dependent conditional temperate variances exist at this site (it can get hot in July) based on the time of day, or the season, or if its a bright sunny windless day, or an overcast breezy afternoon. Until you experience the flavor of Alpenglow you have missed one of the finest bouldering spots this region has to offer.

DIRECTIONS

On the hi-ball *Alpenglow V1*

40 ALPENGLOW BOULDERS • Road and Path Map

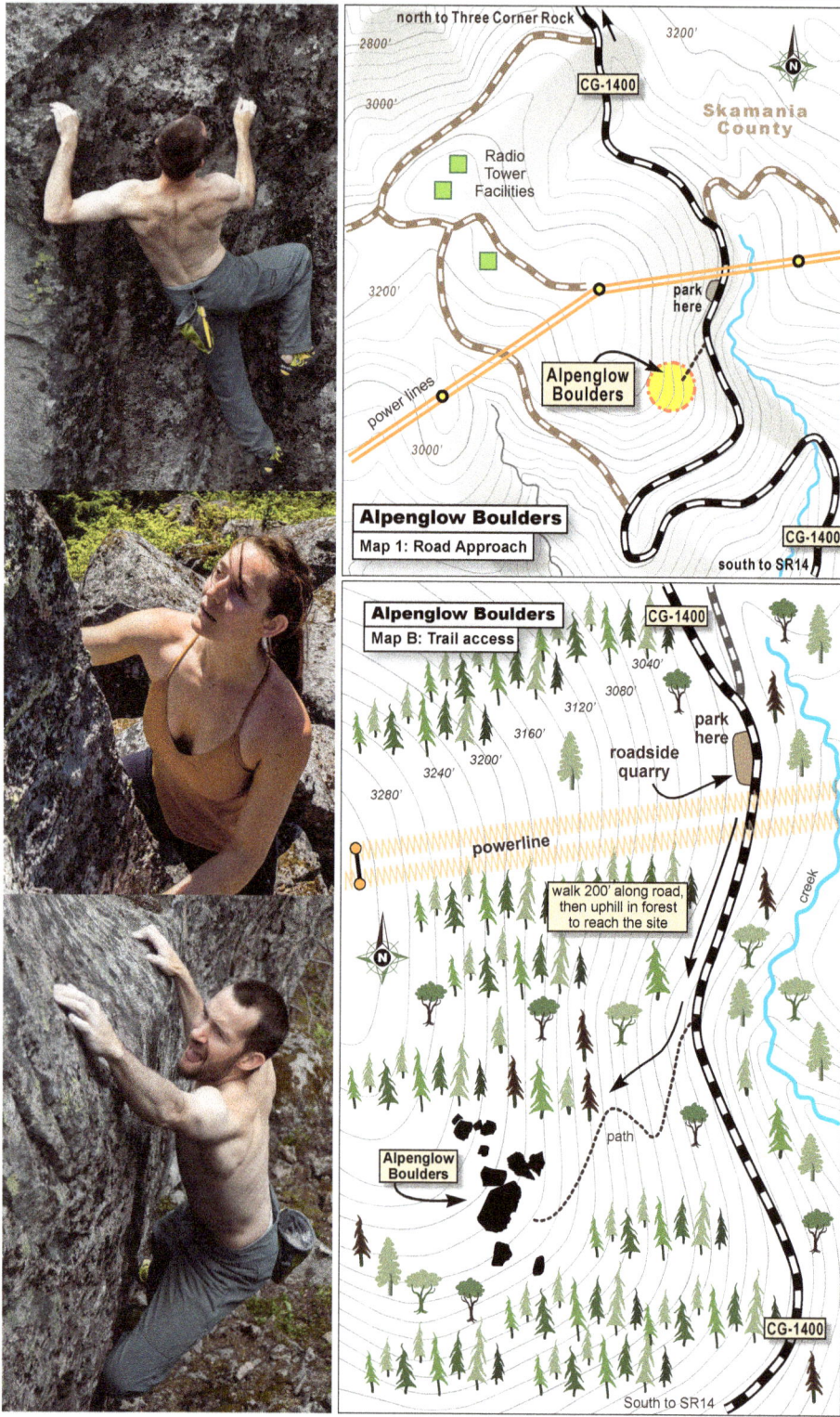

Tymun on *Cathedral Boulder*

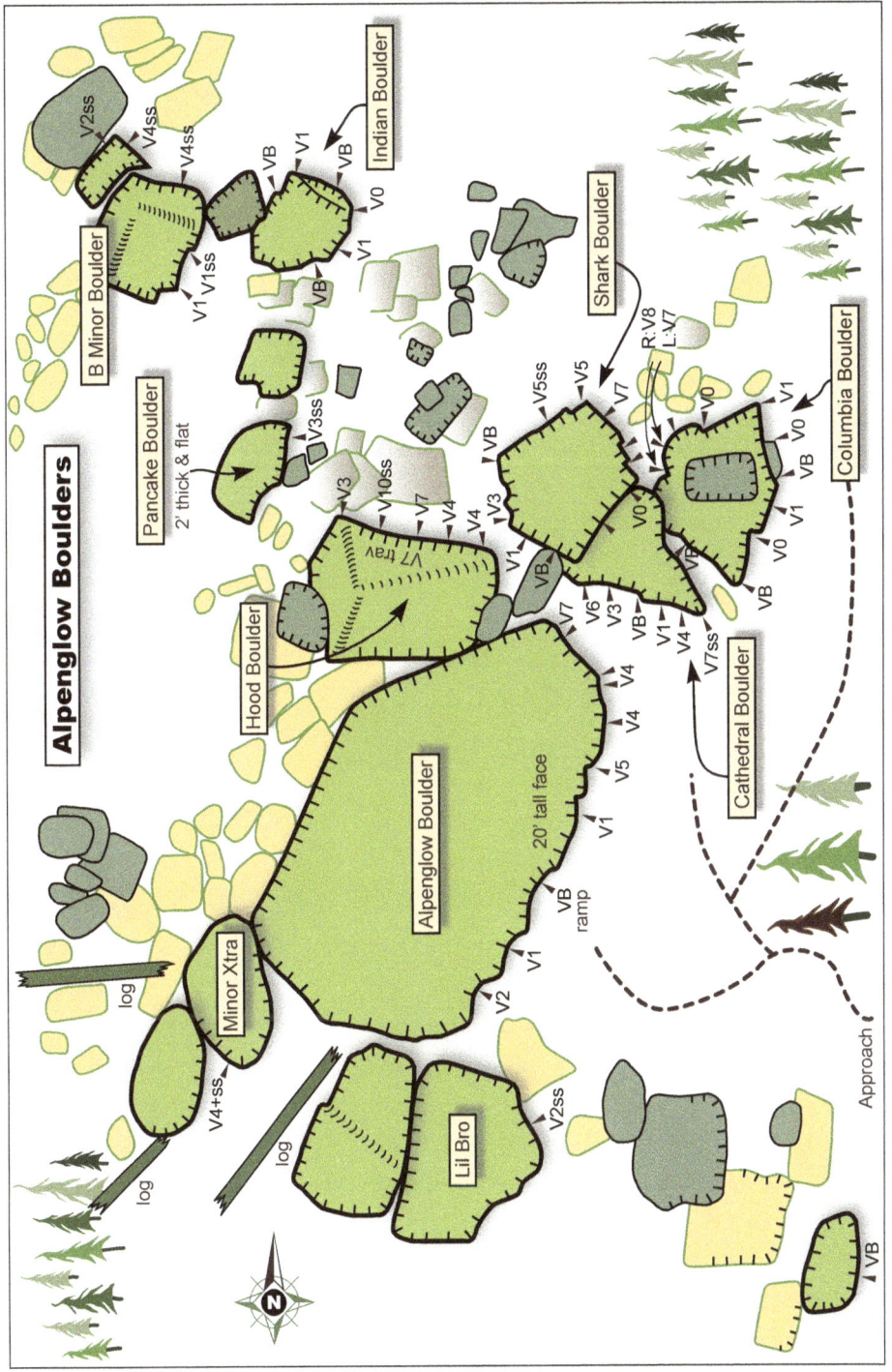

Site Map • GB 41

GPS coordinates for Alpenglow Boulders:
GPS UTM 10t 572881 5058826

42 ALPENGLOW BOULDERS • Alpenglow

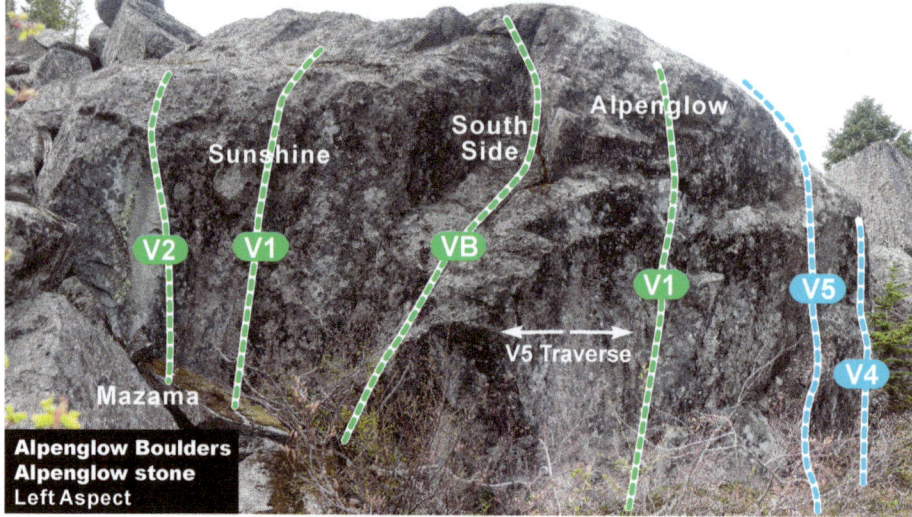

Alpenglow Boulders
Alpenglow stone
Left Aspect

Alpenglow Boulders
Alpenglow stone
Right Aspect

From State Route 14 at Beacon Rock, drive north on paved road Kueffler Road for 2 miles, then of NF1400 road for six miles till you reach the power lines (at a roadside talus quarry). Park in a wide spot there at the quarry, and walk several hundred feet back downhill on the main gravel road, then angle up slope (off-trail scramble) into thick forest aiming for a cluster of stones about 300' above the road.

Alternate: a very long alternate option exists by driving up the entire Washougal River road to the pass, then south

Shane on *Shark Arête*

on a rough gravel road that circumnavigates the west slope of 3-Corner Rock to reach Alpenglow Boulders from the north.

Alpenglow Boulder

This is the big long beast boulder with a string of high quality problems along its SE aspect. The hi-ball Alpenglow line beckons for those who relish savvy with spice. A great spot to warmup and catch a scenic view. Beta is listed from left to right:

V2 Mazama ★★

This is the leftmost problem tucked in the vertical scoop.

V1 Sunshine ★★

The next scoop to the right.

VB Southside ★★ ⚠

A series of small sloped steps and edges leading up into a prominent slot corner near the top.

V1 Alpenglow ★★★★ ⚠

Alpenglow tackles the tall section of the stone in the center of the face using a series of down sloping fat ramp rail edges, then delicately moves past the high rounded bulge onto the slab (hi-ball).

V5 The Spur ★★

Tackles a slight bulge using two tricky downward sloping fat rails (behind a small tree).

V4 Ice Feathers ★★★

This is a quality series of pockets and sidepulls on a slight hung double nose feature.

V4 Sunspot ★★★

This involves crimps to a slight notch at the lip, then follow the seam past the notch onto top slab (a V5 variation also merges into it).

V7ss Bring It On

A techy crimp line on the far right at slot.

THE TRAVERSE:

V5 Alpenglow Traverse ★

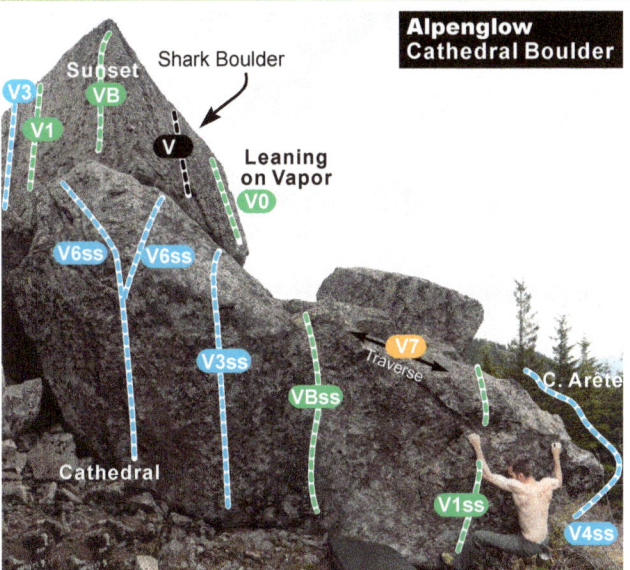

Entire base traverse (exclude the V7ss).

Cathedral Boulder

A long cigar-shaped block with a set of problems facing the sunshine. All short problems, but this boulder has some very cool problems, too. Beta is L to R:

V6 Cathedral ★★

This is a series of rounded slopers. Start at the far left at a nook where the boulders jam together (alternate ending V6 var).

V3ss Heather ★

A face with several tiny crimps.

VBss Bear Grass

A minor shorty groove.

V1ss Lip of Light ★

Start low just left of the next problem using several crimpy features on a short face.

V4ss Cathedral Arête ★★★★

The lower prominent classic overhung nose. SS and punch directly over the entire thing.

THE TRAVERSE:

V7 Cathedral Traverse ★★★

Sit start on the Cathedral Arête, then traverse left uphill to the last problem and top out.

Columbia Boulder

This is a big square-*ish* boulder with a

44 ALPENGLOW BOULDERS • Columbia Boulder

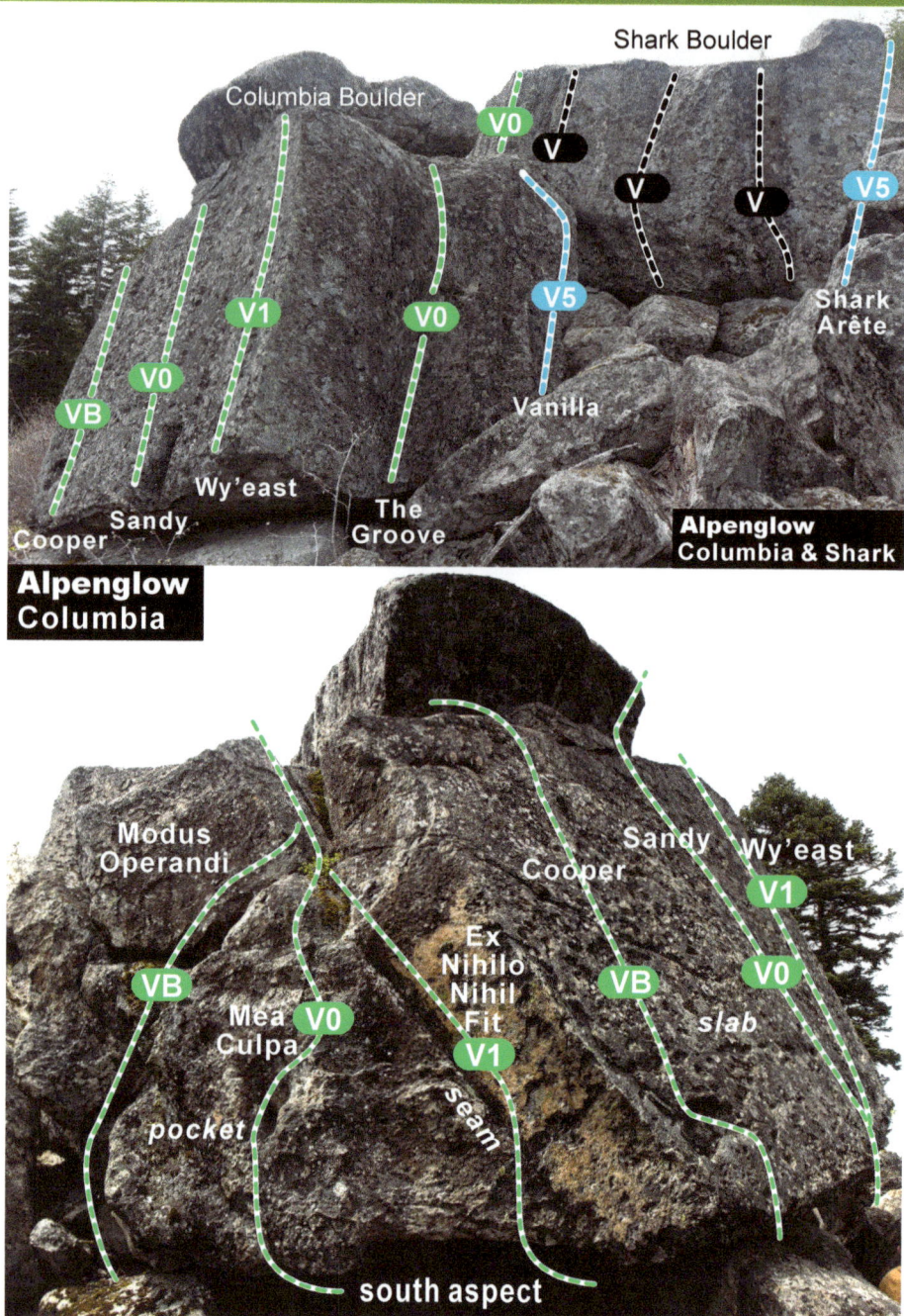

smaller squat block perched on top of it. The east face aspect is a tall hi-ball slab, while the shorter uphill section is tucked in a nook created by a group of blocks. Beta is L to R starting on the lower left end facing Mt Hood:

VB Modus Operandi

March up steps, and minor groove on far left.

V0 (V1ss) Mea Culpa ★★
Use the giant gas pocket. Nice move, but can boost the power by doing a low sit start.

V1 (V3ss) Ex Nihilo Nihil Fit ★★

Shark Boulder • GB 45

Start at overhang using a leftward slanting seam. Can bump up the V by doing low sit.

VB Cooper ★★★ ☐
Start on a small base stone, step onto an incut gas pocket, then cruise up the fun slab run on small pockets.

V0 Sandy ★★★ ☐
The right part of the same tall slab but starting at a slight notch, then cruise up left on the small pockets on the face.

V1 Wy'east Arête ★★★★ ☐
The classic sharp profiled arête which is always worth doing it. Start as previous but use the right hand arête.

V_ (?) _____ ☐
There may be a futuristic line on the face immediately right of the arête on its north side.

V0 The Groove ★ ☐
An obvious minor groove on the north side of the boulder.

V5ss Vanilla ★★ ☐
A short slightly overhung rounded face (using a minor round prow).

V7ss Don the Armoire ★★ ☐
An overhung face tucked in a small nook created by several nearby blocks.

V8ss Don't Sweat the Technique ★ ☐
Tucked deeper into the same deep overhung nook. With left hand on hung rail, power out an overhung roof.

Shark Boulder
This is located just uphill from the Columbia Boulder. This high proudly perched boulder is stacked on part of the Cathedral Stone. The first problem listed below is the basic line on the southwest aspect. Beta is de-

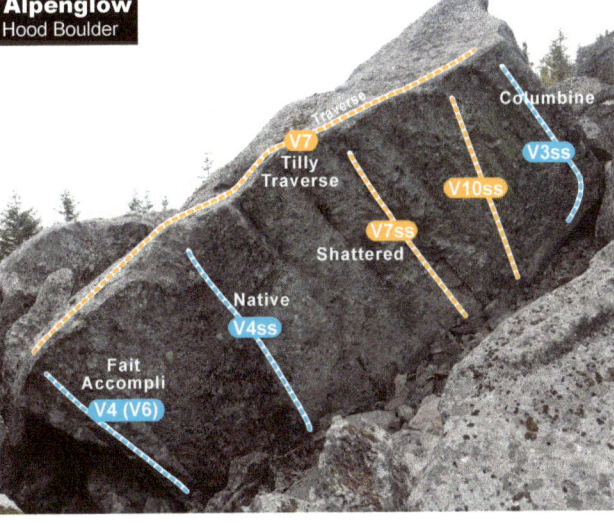

scribed clockwise right to left:

VB Sunset ★

Ascend it by standing on the Cathedral Boulder, make one move up, grab top, and mantle onto summit.

V1ss Northern Lights ★★★

A cool short crimp problem. Climb a slight vertical seam on a flat face.

V3ss Edge of Life ★★

Squeezed in there just left of the previous line. Use your right hand on a sharp lip.

VB Mantle

Just a brief jug mantle.

VB Descent

Well...the descent of course.

V5ss+ (?) _____

A possible corner-*ish* nuance that is tucked in further right of Shark Fin Arête [a block is in the way though].

V5ss Shark Fin Arête ★★★★

The super cool and classic problem that ascends the sharp arête.

V7+ (?) _____

Start on the immediate left side of the previous routes arête, but go up left on crimps to the flat lip.

V7+ (?) _____

Unproven overhung groove on a vertical face.

V8+ (?) _____

Another unproven overhung groove.

V0 Leaning on Vapor

Stand on the Columbia Boulder, and do a high step one-move onto this stone (with a partner as your backup).

V8-9ss+ (?) _____

Down in a pit, is this powerful seriously overhung crimp climb on the east aspect.

Hood Boulder

One of the other great spots to bring a crashing set of pads and work on some ultra power. The beta is left to right.

V4 (V6ss) Fait Accompli ★★

Start low on the far lower left and power up the overhung rib, then over lip.

V4ss The Native ★★★

Start low and make several crimps moves that end on a groove then the lip mantle.

V7ss Shattered ★★

Start low using a sidepull and reach tiny crimps, then catch lip and power over.

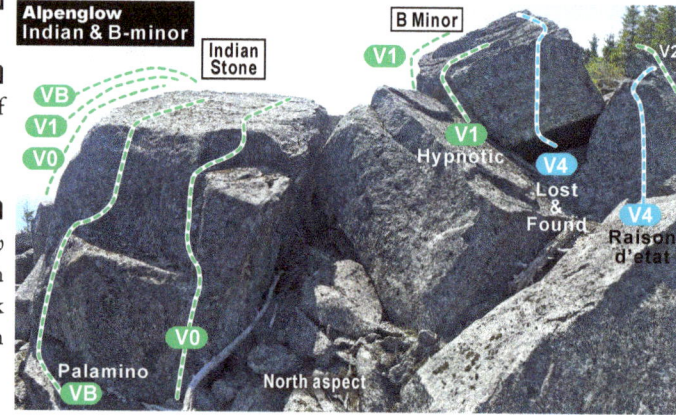

The Minor Stones • GB 47

V10+ss (?) _____
A very thin crimpy face on right half of this boulder (project).

V3ss Columbine ★
Just a nice warmup on a rounded right nose.

THE TRAVERSE:

V7 Tilly Jane Traverse ★ ★ ★
Quality and very powerful slopers rail traverse. Begin on leftmost route down low and run rightward along the entire lip.

Pancake Boulder

Very flat flat boulder, easy to mistake as you wander past it. But yup thars something on it, too.

V3ss Pancake ★
A minor flat 2' thick block with a low traverse.

Indian Boulder

The next several boulders are fairly minor, but a few of the problems offer unique enough variety for the easier grades. Beta is from left to right:

VB Teepee ★
Climb a scoop and keep right hand on a fin.

V1ss Indian Scout ★ ★
Use your left hand on a fin while going up face.

V0ss Peace Pipe ★
A minor rounded face.

VB Palamino
On the north aspect is a series of steps.

V0ss Bring Your Bow
A minor point and rightmost problem.

B Minor Boulder

Tymun on Shark Fin Arête

Shane on Tilly's Traverse

Definitely a small boulder. Beta is listed from left to right:

V1ss Nolens Volens ☐
Ultra low sit, catch lip and up. On SE aspect.

V1ss Hypnotic ☐
Ultra low sit start hold, grab lip, and up (all using low hung prow really). On the SE aspect.

V4ss Lost & Found ★ ☐
Under the lowest part of stone on the north side. Sit start low on a short rail and get up.

C Minor Boulder

And right next to the previous stone is this minor stone. Beta L to R.

V4ss Raison d'etat ★ ☐
Outer steep aspect has a low crimpy sit start problem.

V2ss Hypnosis ☐
And a final minor 'ss' problem on uphill side.

Other Boulder

And way over on the SW upper side of the Alpenglow Boulder is a brief block that got just big enough to yield a minor sit problem.

V4ss _____ ☐
Just sit low and crimp an overhang to the lip and over the top.

Portland's Best Bouldering

4

EMPIRE BOULDERS

The Empire Boulders is certainly the gem quality site Portlander's have been long awaiting to see. Packed into a remarkably compact zone of about 700' square with a wide variety of sizable boulders that are loaded with every rating possible from VB to V-insane (including hi-ball lines) the Empire is truly destined to become a locally popular, highly favored site.

For those folks who prefer nationally famous places like Buttermilk Boulders (or any global bouldering site) this little site is very good. For those who live in this micro-region this site is a cool gem that seemingly fits a miniaturized version of one of those ultra-stellar destination bouldering places. When compared to other bouldering sites in this region few compare with the sheer magnitude of the technical nature, quality, and difficulty found at this one bouldering site.

Empire's combined total number of problems on the boulders and on the bluff outcrop exceeds 300 problems (90% of it tapped by just two persons). The height of many boulders are in that spice and dice range where several crashpads stacked minimize the jump-off gambit.

The bouldering ratings are suitably broad for both entry level boulderers and skilled experts, with plenty of warm-up lines VB-V4, a lesser string of mid-level power lines V5-V8, followed with a select upper string of V9-V12+ futuristic lines. All the boulders tumbled long ago from a minor cliff band just above the dense stone cluster. The bluff offers a plethora of power problems (some substantially overhung) with beastly lines trending upward to 25' tall.

Empire Boulders is easily reached by a convenient paved road to a parking pullout spot (there are residential dwellings nearby so think low-key non-noise environment) and a forested short approach path.

Bring more than one crashpad, especially if you plan to do anything hi-ball. Bring a chalk-bag for your waist especially if you are there on a warm summer day doing hi-ball lines. When the moss regrows you may need to apply a brush to some lines a bit though the many overhung lines will not see much regrowth. Fir needles become a slight nuisance in the spring season so consider bringing a small whisk broom to knock off the excess needles. Certain 18-27' hi-ball boulders and outcrops have a top anchor (or nearby tree) if you desire a top-rope.

HISTORY

Empire is ultra secluded in a forest grotto. It's discovery would have been impossible except for the sleuthing skill of a local mushroom hunter. Therefore, considerable appreciation goes to our close friend Mr. B who stumbled upon this site long ago and kept it secret for many years. He eventually revealed it to Mr O, who, after an additional several years elapsed invited Mr A to the site so that he could get that renewed spark for bouldering. His comment pretty much sums it up, "...I've been waiting a life-time for a place like this near home base." So this exclusive team tapped into the site even more heavily in 2014-2018. These two folks are the highly valued primary site development stewards at this site (as well as many of this regions other sites). Yet there are some untapped lines at EB (albeit hi-ball and extreme power lines). The V9-V12+ lines, though stunning, tend to be few in totality (no more easy sugar cookies).

Sam on B is for Brutus

Stepping briefly back into a historical time frame, it can be noted that for many years Bridge of the Gods Boulders were thought to be charting the next golden age of Portland bouldering. Then, along came a string of gems such as Alpenglow and Three Corner Rock to shake up the scene (if you were part of that inner circle). Then along came Lost Lake Boulders which in its own way is an earth shaking site for this region. Yet all of these places missed just a few minor details; ultra compact site, hi-ball lines with natural soil landings, summer time bouldering in a forested scene (imagine boiling hot days at Hamilton Boulders), gargantuan stone beasts, easily accessible boulders from a paved county road, superb quality stone textural nuances, and virtual all-year bouldering. With a few days of dry weather in the winter this site may be viable even in the winter months. This lengthy combination of unique factors make Empire Boulders this micro-regions prime bouldering site.

In this northwest USA micro-region the boulder size does not necessarily equate to quality boulder problems, but this compact site offers a surprise, in that even the tall V0 sketch lines are crimp/smear adventure spicy problems that can satisfy even the most ardent chalk warrior. So just how big is the biggest stone here? The Roman Boulder is a triangular shaped beast that logs in at 36' x 34' x 28' girth, and 19' tall on its east aspect. OK...super wow! Surprisingly, this yields a rare single massive stone that is both easily accessible and of a quality composition ideal for bouldering (within a short drive of Portland). The tallest single stone is 27' tall (Inca Boulder). The tallest part of the cliff outcrop is over 30' tall.

ROCK TYPE & ROCK NUANCES

The bluff formation and boulders are broadly classed as a pyroclastic or volcanoclastic rock deposit, and was likely laid down under rapid volcanic processes that enhanced the stratified layering effect with heat compaction under pressure. The strata is duo-tone gray welded lithic (e.g. solidified) ignimbrite-*like* ash bed. The strata contains vesicular pockets, small scooped out spheroidal surface weathered divots, distinct internal strati-

fied banding, including considerable embedded fragments of basaltic rock chips of various small sizes, and limited quantities of various scattered minerals such as quartz.

The rock textural nuances are very amenable for bouldering, and offer a well textured friction-friendly surface, some large angular flat aspects, substantial overhung sections, considerable gas pockets of variable sizes (usually rounded but sometimes incut) from micro to 7", small embedded basaltic nubbin protrusions (up to 5") welded into a gray ground mass.

PESKS & OTHER NUISANCES

Yes, there are some. Poison oak exists in very limited spotty places, varieties of flies, horseflies, mosquitoes, spiders, etc., pretty much all the typical things one might find in the forest except gorillas. The flying pests are active primarily in early summer but relatively inactive on cool cloudy or breezy days. Evenings will bring out the mosquitoes. Hornets are a difficult encounter (they give no advance warning) and nests may exist in the general vicinity (use caution when marching off trail). Moss and various dust lichens occur mainly on less traveled boulder problems. And did we forget to mention the bears. If you are bouldering silently for considerable periods, bears may wander unexpectedly through the bouldering area (sing a little jingle if you are there alone).

ADVANTAGES & VARIETY

The site is shaded all year by tall Douglas fir trees, so summer time is quite viable here, even in July so long as there is a breeze. It's a low elevation (1050') site so it seldom gets snowed in, but it can be damp in the winter months, therefore its seasonally viable 12-months of the year *when* its dry. On boiling hot summer days (90°F or higher) that lack a breeze the humidity factor tends to limit your ability to crank V-hard. Contrary to most bouldering sites in this region the Empire Boulders do offer parameters highly favorable to *family-friendly* bouldering outings (approach, some low angle boulders, non-rocky terrain). Cell phone reception is good. Additionally, the site is on US Forest Service managed land.

This is a viable multi-use site offering fall season bouldering, mushrooming, and perhaps minor top-roping. Power is always needed for the crimpy stout lines, but a sustained level of endurance and steady focus is beneficial for the lower grade hi-ball lines. For the low-ball fanatic there are plenty of short lines and traverses to tweak your tips.

GRADES

The boulders yield a suitable range of difficulties conducive to most persons in this sport. The total problems here exceed the 300 goal post. The most common grade of course is V0-V3 (40%); the next most common is VB (30%) [anything 5.0-5.9]; a lesser group of V4-V8 (20%); and only a smattering of extreme V9-V14 problems (10%).

BOULDER NAMES

The ideological naming conventions seen at the Empire Boulders are generally attained from obsolete empires, emperors, dynasties, or autocracies from the various imperialism's of centuries past. And due to a friendly local bear population we dedicated a few stones to the furry black creatures, too. Part of the outcrop bluff formation is broadly named the Great Wall of China with correlating dynasties (or prominent regional features) to pinpoint each specific smaller outcrops. All this and more at a curiously fascinating bouldering site spiked by a wealth of history.

STEWARDSHIP

There are residential dwellings nearby along the primary paved road, so common etiquette is required for long-term viability of this site. Enjoy the quiet forested appeal of the site. Avoid using boombox stereos, keep pets in control (i.e. leashed), use the established path network, bury your pooh in a distant location, etc. You might limit smoking here (a LNG pipeline is located nearby) for everyone's safety. The vine maples around the boulders keep the poison oak from growing too easily, so keeping as much undergrowth growing is vital. The site steward is Mr A; he frequently boulders here with friends, and he often emphasizes site values, promotes safety, user discretion, and courteous interaction. If you send a new line (a rare day here indeed) provide your latest project 'send' info to him, and be of valuable service to this site by assisting the 'caretakers' in various stewardship opportunities at this site.

PATH ACCESS

A brief 800' long path gently ascends an open forested slope passing several smaller stones en route to the Roman Boulder. When you reach this big stone the path splits four ways. A promi-

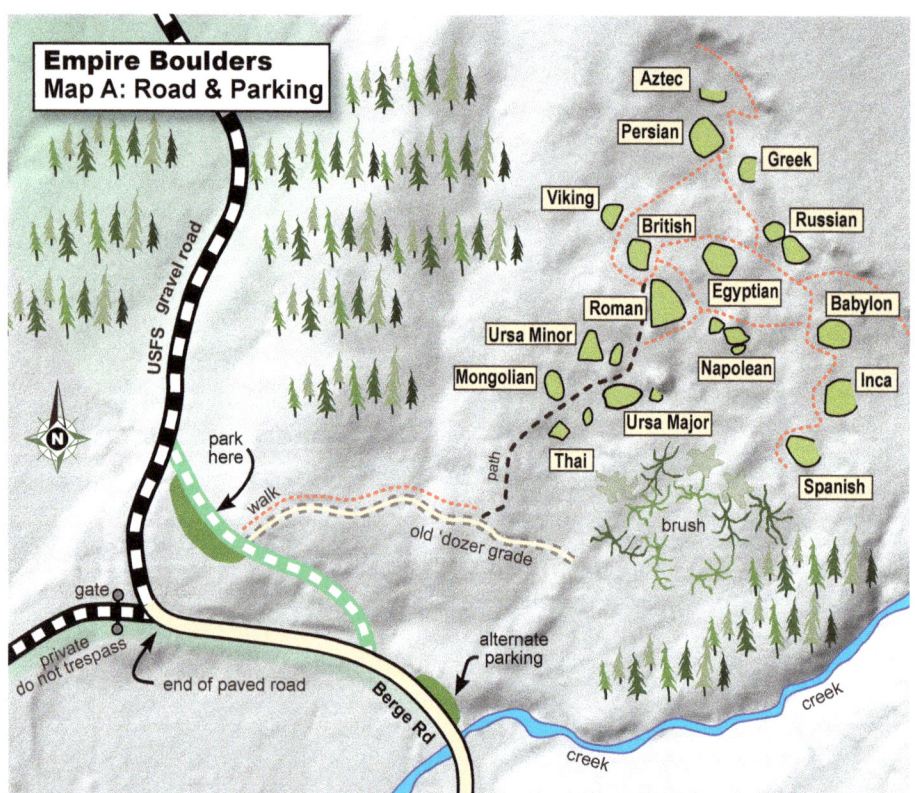

nent deer path ventures NW to the Greek-Persian stones, a NE path trends past Russian stones en route to the bluff, an east path (past Napolean stones) leads direct to Babylon-Inca stones. Some of the forest near the boulders is a tangle of low brush, wind fall, and minor poison oak.

SITE ORIENTATION

This site is encompassed by a long east-west randomly outcropping short bluff. Below this bluff formation the entire group of boulders are found concentrated into generally four primary areas; the initial trail cluster (the Bear Cluster), the central cluster (the Roman Boulder), the upper west cluster (the Greek Boulder), and the east cluster (at the massive Inca Boulder). The site is nicely wrapped in a deep forest canopy of fir trees.

CAMPING OPTIONS

Timberlake Campground and RV Park is located less than one mile down the road, and it offers quality seasonal camping arrangements for those travelers who are on a road bouldering tour of the U.S. west coast region. Another quality seasonal campground is located at the Skamania county baseball park (east end of park). This county park and campground offers riverside access and free shower facilities. The county campground is open from May 1st – Oct 31st . With two very nearby quality camping facilities, do not camp at the bouldering site, nor at the end of the paved road at the parking spot.

AMENITIES

The nearest large grocery store is located in Stevenson, Washington, though a good tiny mart exists at Home Valley (⅛ mile east of Berge Road junction) for basic items. Stevenson also has a variety of shops and fast food arrangements, and is the county seat for administration and emergency services.

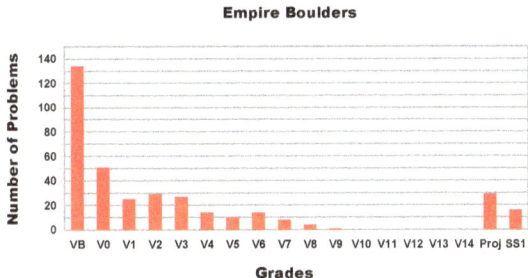

DIRECTIONS

Drive east from Portland, Oregon on I-84 freeway. At Cascade Locks cross the Bridge of the Gods bridge. From the north end of the bridge on State Route 14 continue east (passing Stevenson, WA) for 8.3 miles. When you enter the small community of Home Valley turn left (north) onto Berge Road and drive uphill for 3.6 miles to the end of the paved

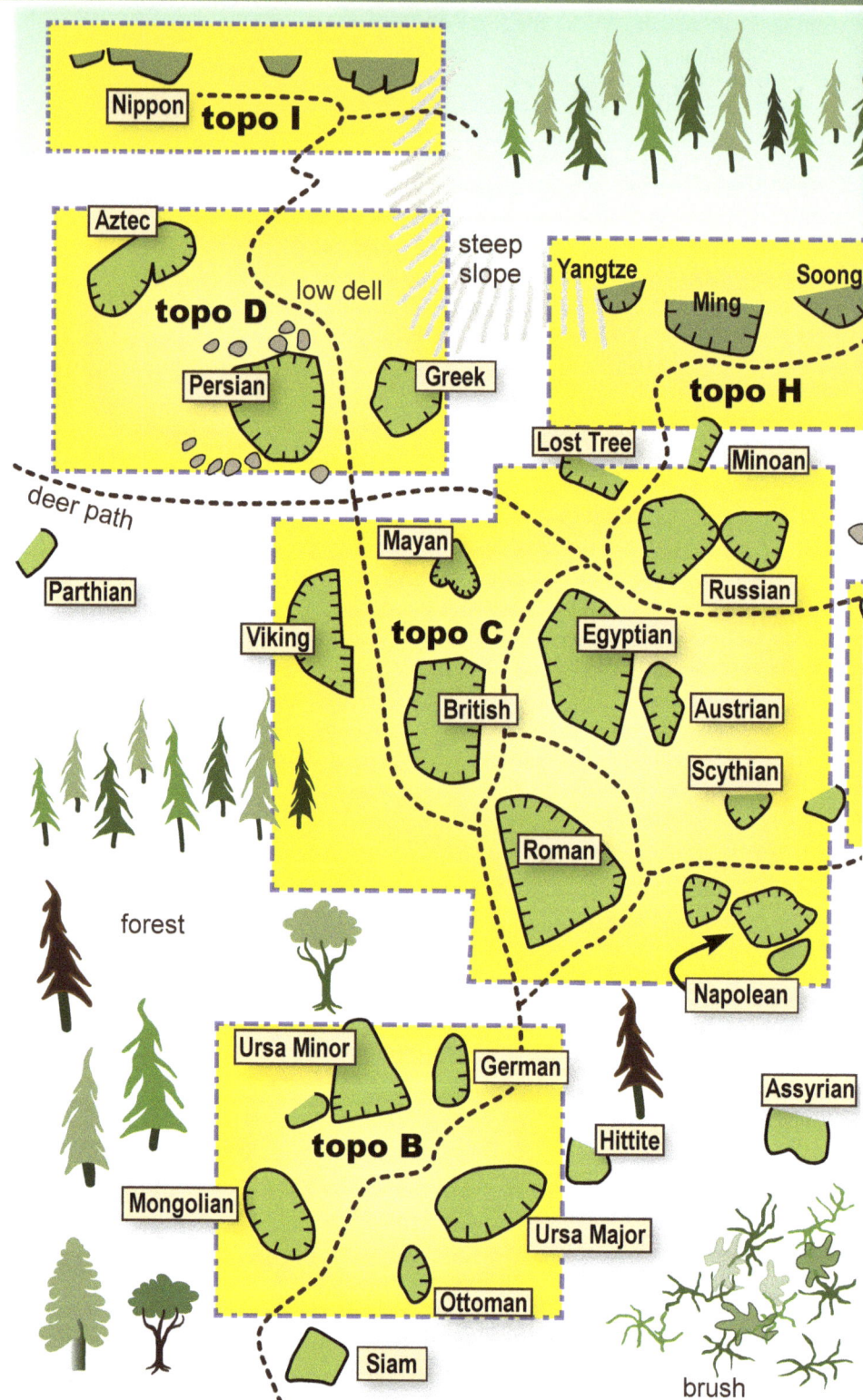

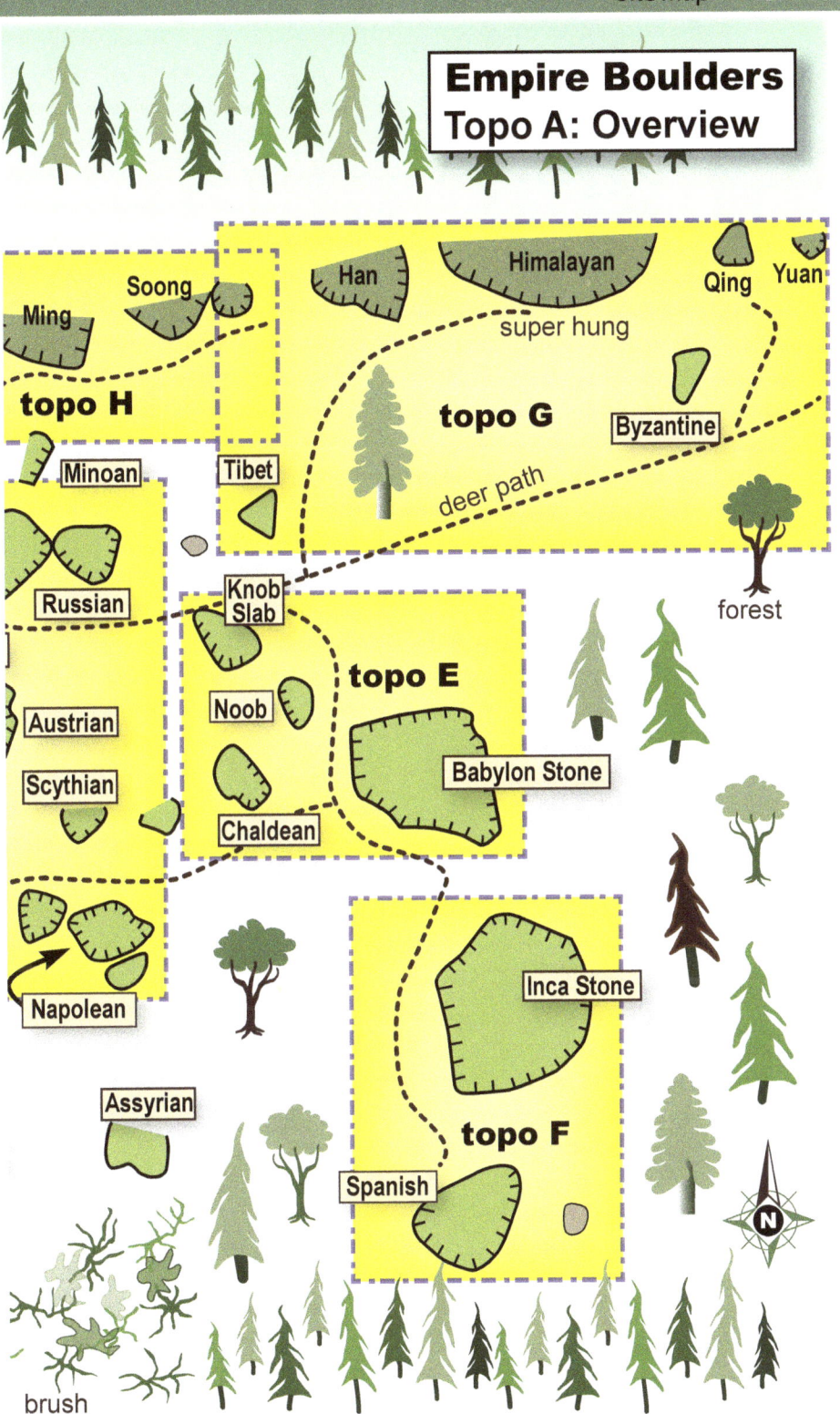

EMPIRE BOULDERS — The Bear Group

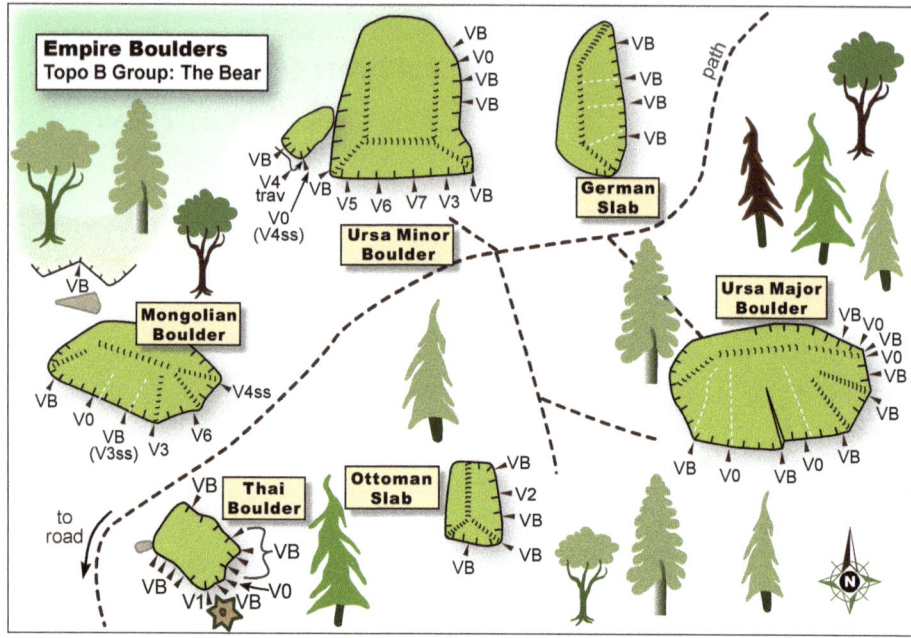

road and park alongside the paved road, or park on a dirt side spur [see map] (do not block the private driveway, nor the USFS road). Walk uphill on a narrow path for about 500' to reach the first boulders. Anticipate about 1¼ hours drive time from Portland-Vancouver. The GPS coordinates at the end of the paved road is UTM 10t 596190 5066379.

THE BEAR GROUP

The Bear Cluster is the first series of six boulders that range in height from disgustingly short to invitingly tall, yet each seems to have quantitative gems certain to wet your palette. So, let's begin this famous site tour with our first stone, the Pax Mongolia.

Mongolian Boulder

This is the initial minor low laying oval-shaped boulder with an obvious sloped lip wrapping around its south aspect. Its the first stone you encounter walking up the path en route to the main area. Beta is Left to Right:

VB Ultima Ratio Regum (aka War) ☐
Minor problem; easy get down method.

V0ss Mandate from Heaven ★ ☐
Brief small crimps over lip onto slab.

VB (V3ss) Khublai Khan ★★ ☐
Fat hold mantle. Sit start adds a long lunge.

V3ss Hwacha ★★★ ☐
Crimps at the lip, and a tough dead-point to reach crimps on the slab face above.

V6ss The Scourge ★ ☐
Start on two sloper edges, use lip moving right up over the very point of overhang.

V4ss Genghis Khan ★★ ☐
Start very low on left pocket and right side pull, then lunge for the jug, and power mantle over the lip yield a superb line.

Siam Boulder (aka Thai (Siam) Boulder

Technically, this is the first boulder on the hike uphill, though due to its low profile its easy to walk past it without realizing that a few lines exist on the east aspect. It's situated about 30' downhill from the Mongolian Boulder just east of the trail. Beta is L to R:

V1ss Siamese Twin ★ ☐
Low bulge left of the fir tree.

VB White Elephant ★ ☐

Brief flat face just right of a fir tree.

V0 Little Buddha ★

Also just right of tree (very close to left VB) but more on the subtle round point.

VB Red Curry
A short vertical scoop.

VB King and I
A short vertical face.

VB Angkor Wat
Brief east point.

VB Sticky Rice
Odd traverse along north slab.

VB Kneejerk
Minor kick on the north point.

The south aspect has four very short family/kid friendly VB's (2 smear, 2 mantle).

Ursa Minor Boulder

The next substantial sized boulder on the hike uphill. Its a superb 13' tall trail-side stone that has a vertical south-facing aspect with a treasure of serious problems on it. The first beta is for the independent round low blob on the far left. Beta is left to right:

VB Bear Rug
Minor variant on far left.

V4ss Bear Claw ★★★
Traverse from left all the way right into the V0 and then bump up and mantle over bulge.

V0 (V4ss) Chubby Huckster ★★★
Low 'ss' on left dish & crimp, then bump to next crimp, then catch lip, then mantle. The standing start merely starts on both good crimps and bumps for the lip and mantles over.

...And on the vertical south face of the main big boulder (beta is L to R):

VB Pocket Rocket
Use the obvious natural pocket on nose.

V5 Bear Minimum ★★
Left face using a sloped pocket and reaches for more sloped holds.

V6 Big For Your Boots ★★★★
Center power line – pinches, balance, deadpoint reaches.

V7 Three Bears
Power line in the center of face cruising a partial seam.

V3 Bearly There ★★★
Skinny face on the right with surprisingly subtle holds.

VB Bear Facts ★★
Right nose doing just one-two move.

...And on the east side of this same large stone is some family-friendly stuff.
VB a brief face left of crack.
VB **Bear Bait** is the crack on a slab.

V0 Bearvilla. A thin rounded face on a slab.

VB Grin & Bear It. Low angle ramp.

While standing on the path looking up at Ursa Minor Boulder, directly downhill you will find the two following boulders.

Ottoman Boulder

A small minor east-facing slab located about 25' below the path. Beta is L to R:

VB ___
The short leftmost steps.

VB Stairway
Steps and jugs on a nose.

VB ___
A short face.

V2 LP ★★★
This is a quality yet tricky pure smear slab line well worth doing (facing east).
VB short round right face.

Ursa Major Boulder

Large 24' tall stone with a substantial south-facing slab. Located 30' below path. Beta is left to right:

VB Lost Art ★
Nice brief line below the big fir tree on far left.

V0 Bear's Lair ★★ ⚠
A quality skinny opening crux section on a long smear slab.

VB Backwardia-to-Richonia ★★ ⚠
The prominent central sloped trough creates a popular hi-ball fun run.

V0 Divide & Conquer ★★ ⚠
Tackles the hi-ball face and has a skinny crux at mid-height. Cool fun run.

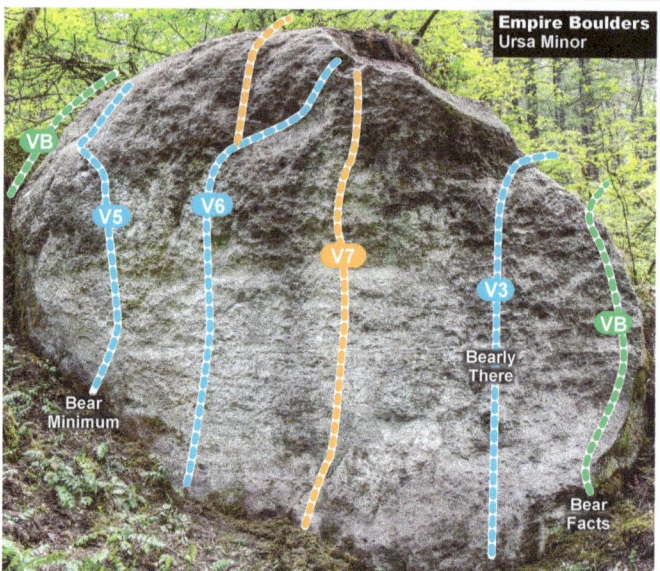

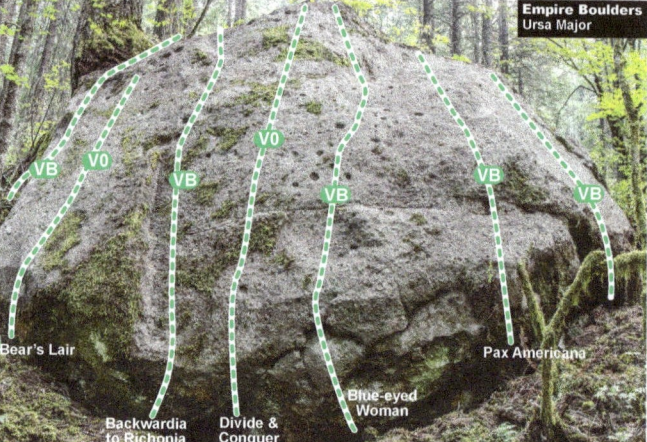

VB Left-handed Blue-eyed Woman ★★ ⚠
Series of prominent pockets make for a fine fun run on long slab.

The following are on the eastern part of the Ursa Major boulder.

VB Pax Americana ★
This is a minor blunt rib on a slab.

VB Bondage
This is a minor series of edges and steps on the far right. On east part of stone.

V0 Spoofed ★★
Quality very short east prow (rules by staying on face) starts with left hand on sidepull.

German / Roman Boulder • GB 59

VB Eulachon
East steps to smear slab (plus variation).

V0 Git Lost
One move face onto a north facing slab.

VB Pax Europa
Low angle slab on north side.

Hittite Boulder

A brief ultra low boulder a few yards east of previous (Ursa) boulder. Four lines (L to R). **VB Kitty** (face), **VB Cool Cat** (one-move crack), **VB Dog** (slab), **VB Pony** (one-move onto right slab). No photo.

German Boulder

This is the minor trail-side low angle eastern-facing slab stone. All four problems are VB (including a cross-all-routes variation). A quality family and kids friendly low angle slab. Beta is left to right:

VB Eagle Claw
This is a left slanted groove.

VB Gothic Art
This is the shorter central face.

VB Boar's Tusk
This is the taller central face.

VB Berlin
And doing just the right rib.

CENTRAL BOULDER CLUSTER

This concentrated and popular spot entails four massive boulders and four smaller stones, primarily wrapped around the famous Roman Stone. Its the area where you will likely hike to first in order to get a quick taste of the power, punch and quality this little site has to offer. The primary approach path splits from this cluster of stones, one path traveling northwest (to the upper west grotto), one path travels northeast (up to the deer path), and a brief path travels southeast to a small set of two minor stones.

Roman Boulder

This is the prominent really big boulder you encounter when the trail lands at a compact cluster of boulders. The Roman Boulder is the *tour-d-force* at EB with everything from mundane to absolutely extraordinaire. This large stone offers a host of quality 360° bouldering. The path directions to reach the remaining stones in the area are coordinated from this major stone. Beta starts at the north point and is described clockwise:

VB Empirical Dreams ★★
The north point fun run and often used as the down climb. This is the *first* line established on the Roman Stone and at the Empire.

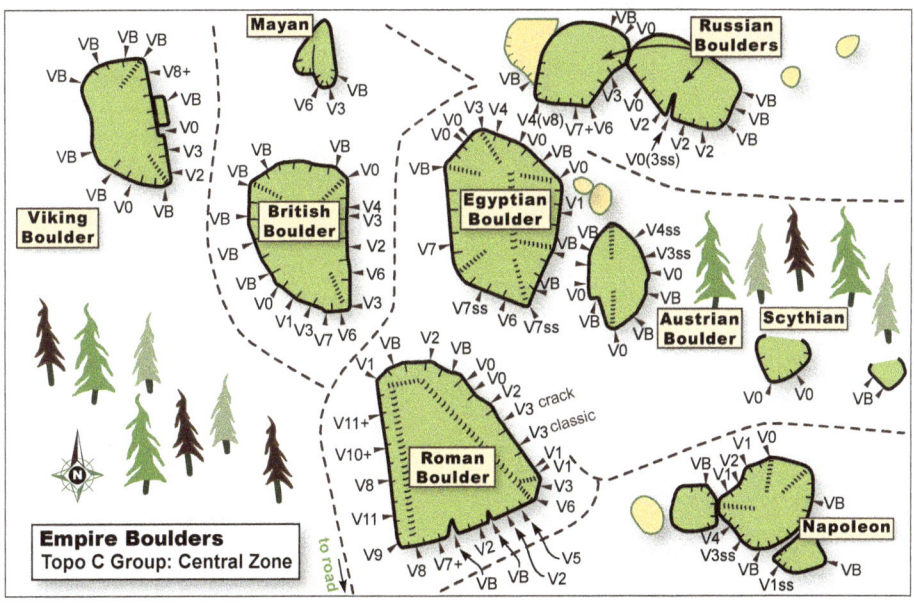

Empire Boulders
Topo C Group: Central Zone

60 EMPIRE BOULDERS • Roman Boulder

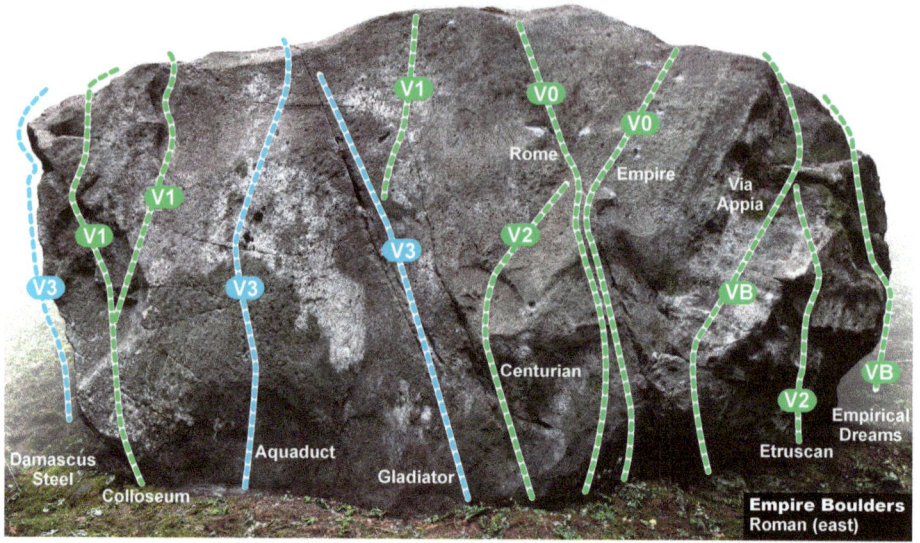

Empire Boulders
Roman (east)

Empire Boulders
Roman (south)

Empire Boulders
Roman (west)

V2 (V3ss) Etruscan ★★★ ☐
Several short enjoyable variants on a slight overhang (all end the same on next VB).

VB Via Appia ★★ ☐
Goes up easy steps; viable as a down climb.

The next six are 18' hi-ball problems.

V0 The Empire ★★★★ ⚠ ☐
Classic. First half of seam then right face. Start up the leftward angling seam till you reach mid-height, then aim up right on smears.

V0 Rome ★★★★ ⚠ ☐
Ultra classic full angled seam. Start at a large pocket on a slight bulge at seam, then go leftward up the seam to the top.

V2 Centurion ★★★ ⚠ ☐
This starts at the crack, pulls the initial bulge using a large pocket then angles up right crossing Rome and finish on The Empire (or finish on the Rome route).

V3 Gladiator ★★★ ⚠ ☐
The prominent center crack. Crimps till the crack widens at mid-height, then balanced movement to finish. Crack can be lead with small stoppers and cams.

V1 Gladiator (Var.) ⚠ ☐
Start same as Gladiator crack but bust up right as an ending variant.

V3 Aqueduct ★★★★ ⚠ ☐
Ultra classic at Empire. Tiny crimpy pocket moves to attain large mid-face pockets, then dicey moves to finish. Way to go Mr A!

V1 Colosseum ★★★ ⚠ ☐
Crux opener move to sloped stance, then calmly reach up left to jug, then jug again.

V1 Colosseum Direct ★★ ⚠ ☐
The same crux opener move to sloped stance, then reach up right to catch a sloped rail and a big flat jug. Pull past the jug to the top.

V3 Damascus Steel ★★★ ⚠ ☐
A superb 17' hi-ball line using an inner scoop of the overhung southeast prow utilizing good crimps and holds (if merged right near top into Colosseum it's V2). Cool discovery Sam!

V6/V7 Ritual Union ★★★★ ⚠ ☐

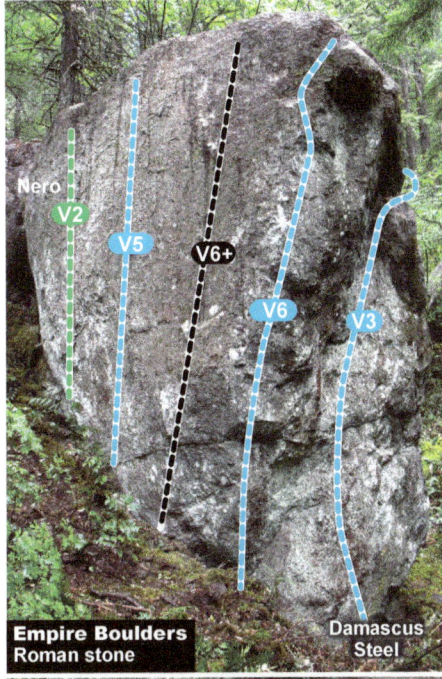

Empire Boulders — Roman stone

Empire Boulders — Roman (north)

Tall overhung blunt prow with a series of unique holds and crimps. A classic and bold hi-ball problem.

The next set of problems are all on the south aspect of this boulder.

V5-7 Vesuvius ☐
Short vertical face with skinny skinny smears (project).

V5 Via Delarosa ☐

Empire Boulders
British (south)
VB
V0
V1
V3
V7
V6
Notre Dame
sit start undercling
sit start
England
Mini Cooper
Quasimodo

V6
V3
V6
V2
V3
V4
V0
sit hold
Quasimodo
Bulldog
Crusade
King Arthur
Excalibur
Empire Boulders
British (east)

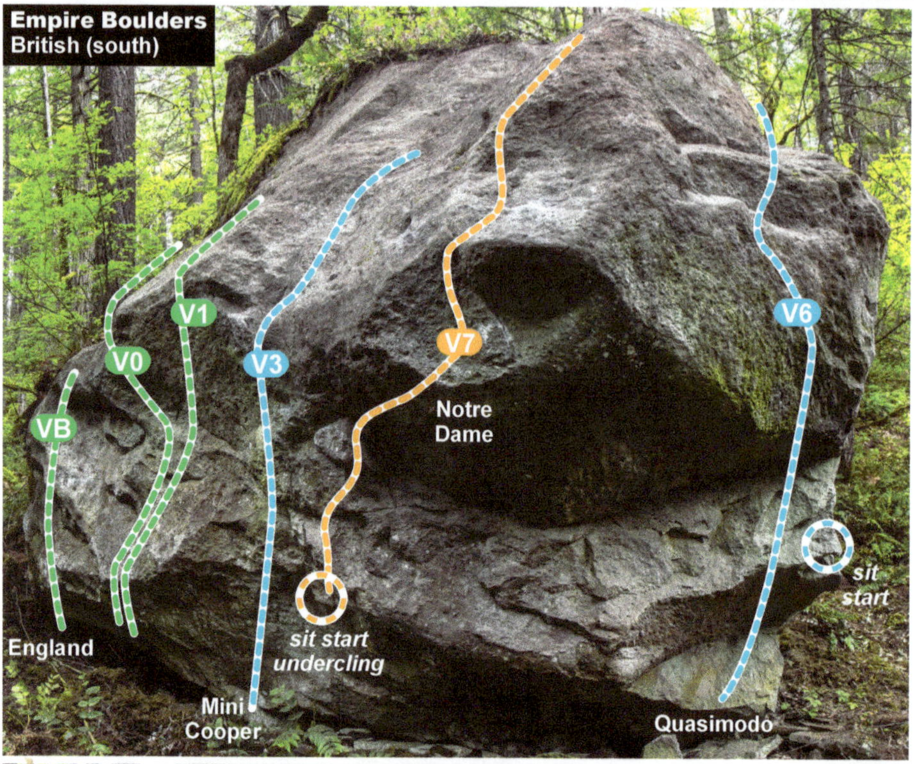

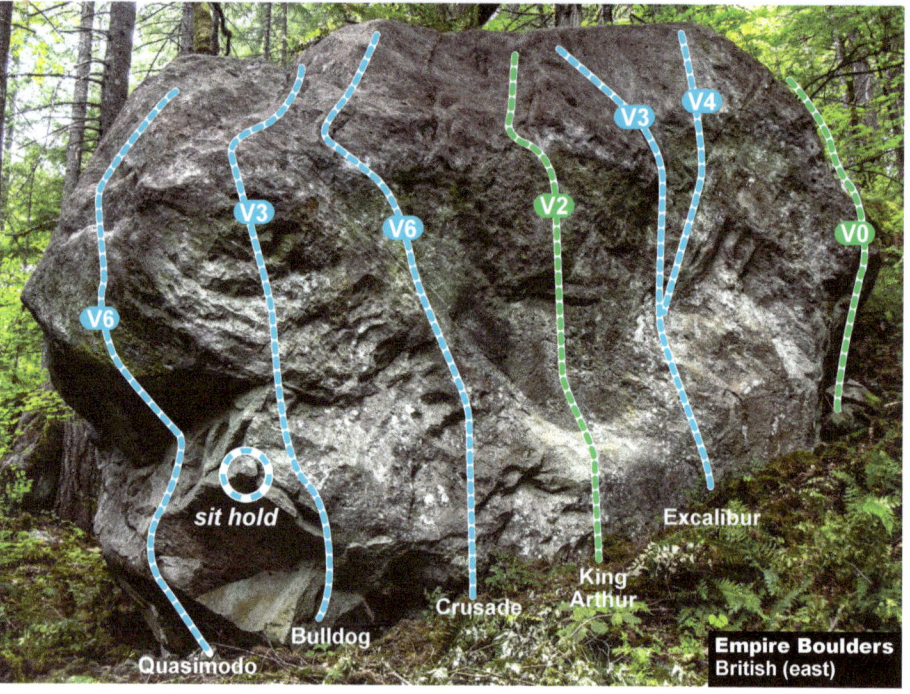

Roman & British Boulder • GB 63

Start on two small pockets, one for each hand.

V2 Nero ★
Thin short face with a few pockets.

VB Preston's Nemesis
Corner-*ish* nuance.

V2 Cobblestone ★★
Everything on short face with pockets.

VB The Scramble
The walk up and walk down.

V8+ Prima Facie
Thin crimps just left of the down scramble. Project.

V9 Architect ★★★
The right aspect of prominent overhung prow on tiny crimps & slopers. V8 if you got beta.

Five futuristic lines exist on the main west aspect of Roman Stone...and these are:

V9 Gladius ★★★★
Overhung technical round arête prow. Crimps to catch high sloper. This has an alternate 'sit start' right start (V9ish) with several power moves and then merges at the fat sloper.

V11 Caesar Salad
Technical crimps face moves to a high sloper rail then into a slight groove at the top.

V7 (V8ss) B is for Brutus ★★
Overhung technical face. Standing start on high crimp and pop for sloped jug. The 'ss' uses a left low undercling. Nice send Sam!

V10+ ____
Tiny crimps and undercling pocket to knob on rail, and into groove at top.

V11+ ____
Overhung face with marginal crimp features.

V1 Spartacus ★★
Minor shorty just right of the standard north point *Empirical Dreams* line. As rated V1 Sparticus Left (use left fingers in seam), and V2 Sparticus Right (is all crimps).

British Boulder

The Anglo-Saxon boulder has a broad rounded prow on the south end, and a slightly overhung flat face on the east side. Beta L to R starting on the far west face:

VB Left Coast
A brief move and mantle (+ minor var).

VB The Real & The Ideal ★
Go up a brief round rib (use or avoid pocket).

VB Boulderville
Basic slab run just right of rib.

VBss Cosmic Order
Low bulge mantle onto easy slab.

VBss England ★★★
Just sit start low and reach over bulge high to grab giant gas pocket and pull up over.

V0 Balance of Power ★★★
Undercling pinch, high right smear, move up left to grab the giant 4" pocket.

V1 British Isles ★★
Start on same undercling pinch (as previous line), high right smear, then move up right directly over the bulge on just crimps.

V3 Mini Cooper ★★★
Overhung face using crimps directly up a seam. Start low on a good right hand crimp and a small left hand crimp.

V7 (V8ss) Notre Dame ★★★★
Start left hand side pull and right hand on good right side pull. Substantially overhung bulge with tenuous reach. Low start uses the undercling.

V6 (V7ss) Quasimodo ★★★★
Hung prow. Start under bulge, power to flat crimp.

And on the east face of this same boulder:

V3 Bulldog ★★★★
The right side of an overhung prow starts by using underclings and a knob hold to reach better holds.

V6 Crusade ★★★
Powerful slightly hung thin face. Start with low right hand crimp pinch and dyno for the high sloper.

V2 King Arthur ★★★
Start at center of boulder below two underclings and climb straight up to the top.

V3 Excalibur ★★ ☐
Uses two small undercling sidepulls, but exit left using natural rail and committing top out.

V4 Excalibur (direct) ★★★ ☐
Start same as previous using the two small undercling sidepulls but continue directly up a blank section with a few reachy high pockets.

V0 Badge of Honor ★★ ☐
Minor seam going over a brief bulge.

VB Fabric of Deceit ☐
Face going over bulge (rightmost line).

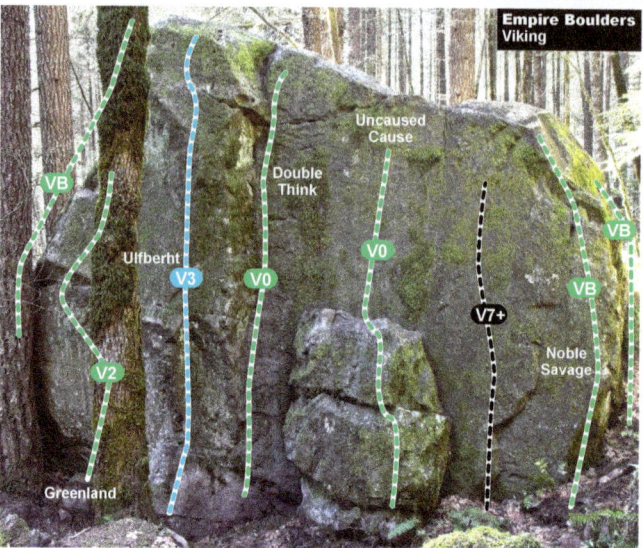

Viking Boulder

Immediately NW of the British Stone another 25' is the Viking Stone which has a sheer east face about 16' tall. Beta is left to right starting on its west side:

VB Raven's of Odin ☐
West face angled slab.

VB False Peace ☐
Brief moves going up left onto slab.

V0 Force Majeure ★★ ☐
Smears on face with small sloper holds.

VB Tectonic Shift ☐
Obvious step prow next to tree.

V2 Greenland ★★★ ☐
Vertical face between two trees. Crimps to jug rail, then a side pull.

V3 Ulfberht ★★★ ☐
Tall prow with long committing reaches.

V0 Doublethink ★★ ☐
Vertical corner that steps up onto the stacked blocks, then several minor moves in the right facing corner to top out.

VB Uncaused Cause ☐
Get onto a stacked block, then mantle the short face above.

Cody on Notre Dame

V8-9[?] ___ ☐
A skinny face with improbable holdless features maybe.

VB Noble Savage ★ ☐
The minor face at NE nose.

VB Cultural Suicide ☐
Minor short face merging left.

VB Standard Bearer ☐
Minor short rounded north face.

Mayan Stone

A minor short slanted hung prow-like stone a few yards uphill from Brit Stone with a few intriguing lines on it. Beta R to L.

VB Chai Frappuccino ☐
The east side shorty.

V3ss Sclerotic Stagnant Superstate ★

Crimp prow, move up right onto slab.

V6 Downtown Funky Stuff ★

Crimps & palm on left side of prow to lip and mantle exit.

Egyptian Boulder

About 30' northeast of the Roman Boulder is the Egyptian Boulder, a tall, yet roughly pyramidal shaped beast with a long slab on its west aspect with a slight overhang to start each problem. Beta runs clockwise starting with the easy lines on the east side:

VB Cheops ★★

The basic up/down line on the east side.

VB Hatshepsut ★

Another basic up/down line on east side.

V8ss Chi Jin Yu ★

Full under prow utilizing incut holds, power out and up. Ends at head height by merging into the previous VB. This is right of fir tree.

V6 Ancesters Protect Me ★★★

Left of fir tree. Start on smooth face, utilize a sidepull undercling to make a long reach.

V7ss Only God Forgives ★★★

Sit low on left in hung nook, cruise several incut holds rightward, then up using a slight crimp and a very long reach over a round bulge.

V7ss Magpie Moments

On round overhung nose is a crux sequence using a small knob.

VB Hieroglyph ★

Easy steps up onto the slab, then run the center of the easy slab.

V0 Sand of the Sahara ★★

Traverse lip leftward, then use the crack with your left hand to surmount the bulge.

V0 Sphinx ★

The jam crack straight on over lip.

V3 Valley of the Kings ★★★

Using the crack with your right hand, move left along the lip, around to north aspect, then surmount the north side of the hung prow.

Empire Boulders
Egyptian (west)

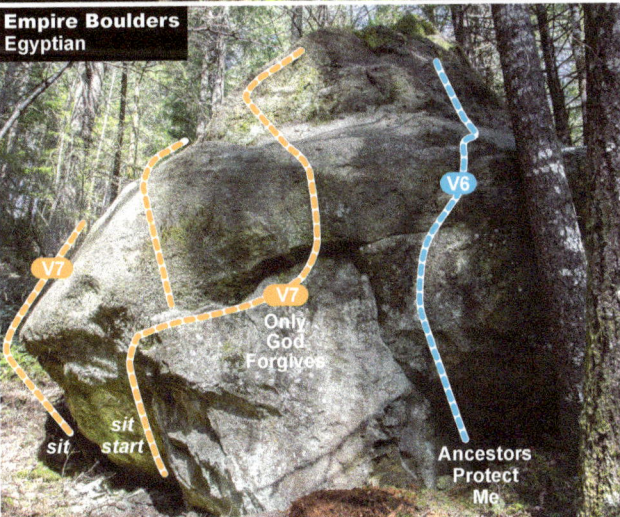

Empire Boulders
Egyptian

66 EMPIRE BOULDERS • Egyptian / Austrian Boulder

V4 King Tut ★★★ ☐
Cool direct start with long reach on north aspect of hung prow.

V0 Pounding Sand ★★★ ☐
Climb up using the grand 7" diameter pocket.

VB Giza ☐
Face-crack next to a detached flake.

V0 State Of DeNile ★ ☐
East prow (and large crack of detached block).

V1 Pharaoh ★★★ ☐
Quality face with small crux crimps (rules avoid crack on right).

THE TRAVERSE:

V6 The Nile ★ ☐
The north side traverse (R to L) starting on the Sphinx problem.

Austrian Stone

A minor block on the immediate east side of the Egyptian Stone. Beta is listed left to right:

VB Slab (short slab on westside) ☐

VB Alps ☐
Short face crack with incuts.

V0 All Things Nice ☐
Brief vertical face on west side.

VB Symphony ★ ☐
Steep corner steps on the west side.

V0 Last Waltz ☐
High step getting onto the south nose.

VB One Move ☐
Short one-move onto slab face.

VB Globalize Me ☐
Doing just the east ramp.

V0 (V2ss) Renaissance ★★ ☐
Brief vertical face on east side starting with hand in the pocket.

V3ss Tic Tac ★★ ☐
Good quality crimps problem utilizing a series of sloper crimps and a slap finish.

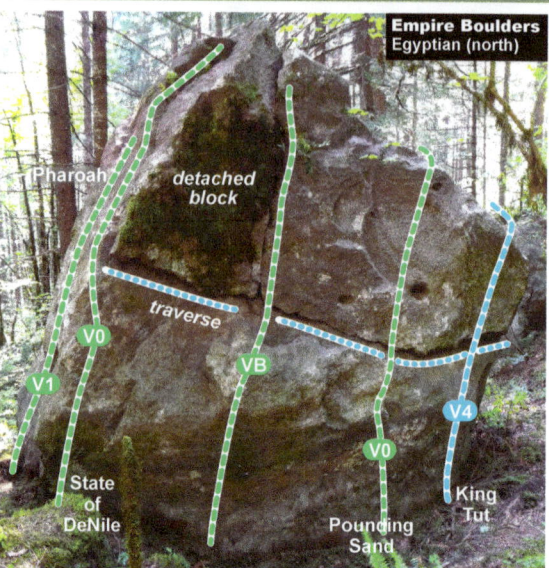

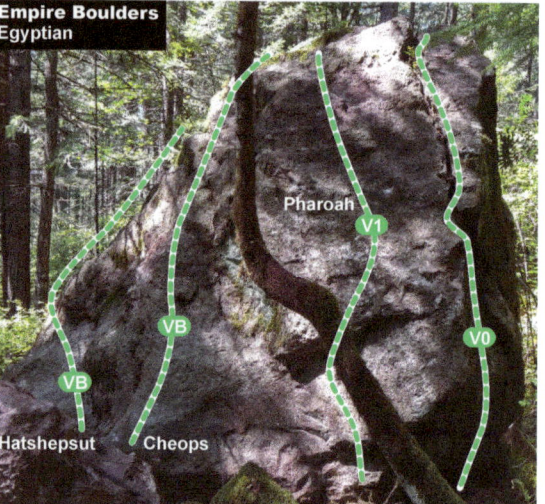

V4ss Little Red Monster ★ ☐
A series of punchy short right facing sidepulls on the east side.

Russian Boulders

Uphill NE of the Egyptian Boulder is this double set of impressive stones. Beta is left to right (starting on the left big boulder):

VB Urals ☐
A short move on far left side.

V4 (V8ss) Kremlin ★★★ ☐
Outer left overhung nose above block. Pinch start and power up to reach a good edge.

V7-8 Vodka Queen ☐
A hard send on the overhung face using an insipient seam (project).

V6 (V7ss) Natasha ★★★ ☐
The first V6 established at the site (way to go Mr A). Start on the boulders inner aspect on two small gaston's and move up a short crimpy face to small sloped holds. V7ss eliminate begins the same spot and goes up right to finish.

V3 Czar ★★★ ☐
Scooped face using left undercling pinch and high reach to catch small crimps.

And on the big right boulder:

VB Volga ☐
The deep wedge slot between both blocks.

V0 Mockba (aka Moscow) ★★★ ☐
Vertical short flat face on the right block.

V2 Ikon ★★★ ☐
Power up a jutting prow just left of a deep overhung OW crack.

V0 (V3ss) Gulag ★★ ☐
The OW crack itself is a viable challenge especially if you sit start it.

V2 Caviar ★★★ ☐
Start about 4' right of crack very low, traverse left upward on positive lip holds (the original line is harder (V3) - missing foot flake). The quality and cool V2ss direct begins with left hand in OW and right on undercling, then punch up right merging into Caviar.

V2 Russian Bear ☐
Start same as previous line, but mantle right over onto slab.

VBss Dr Zhivago ☐
Kids stuff. Left edge of crack. Far east side.

VBss Politburo ☐
Kids stuff. The short crack. Far east side.

The following two problems are on the north side of the boulders.

V0 Siberia ☐
A nice crimp smear line.

Sarah on *Empirical Dreams*

VB Russophobia
Basic short slab move.

Minoan Boulder

A brief low boulder just uphill from the Russian Boulders.

VB King Crossis
Basic low traverse.

History Boulder

VB Scrapheap of History
A minor face with a big fir above it (about 15' NE of Minoan Stone).

Lost Tree Boulder

Brief boulder with short vertical face (about 15' left of Russian Boulder). Beta is R to L:

V1ss Sleepy Salamander ★
Immediately right of the tree on rounded face.

V0 (V4ss) John Deere ★
Start on crimps with foot near a flake (left of tree).

V2ss Minimum Bark
Undercling right, reach high with left.

V2ss Flakey Flake
Brief crimps. Leftmost shorty.

Napoleon Boulders

Also known as the **French Boulder**. About 35' southeast of the Roman Boulder is this a triple set of short boulders nested low in a bowl. Beta is left to right starting on the north side:

VB Arch De Triumph
Minor move left onto a fat stance, then up a short slab face on crimps.

V1 The 1812 Overture ★★★
Tackles a vertical round nose straight on, cul-

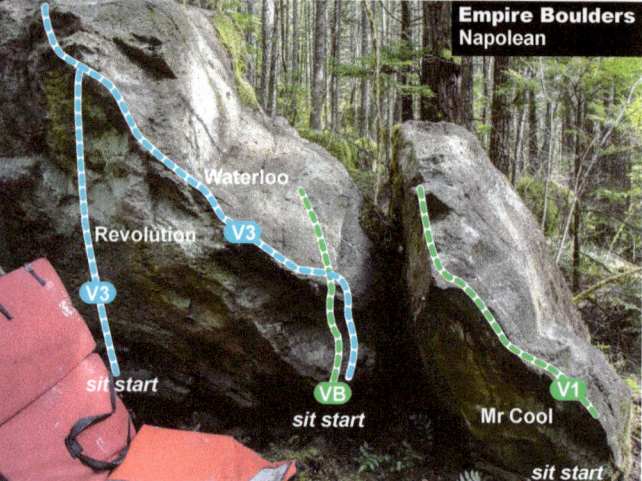

minating with an interesting top out finagle.

V2 Esprit de Corps ★★
Start in the overhung scoop, move up to catch the obvious flat rail, then go straight up over.

V1 Boreas Rising ★★
Start in the overhung scoop, catch the obvious flat rail, then move right to exit up right.

VBss Last Waltz
The low minor step on a short west stone.

On the south side of the same big boulder (beta left to right):

V3ss Revolution ★★
The direct start of the next problem.

V3ss Waterloo ★★★★
Start low on right, cruise leftward and up rounded prow, hand wrap and bounce up the

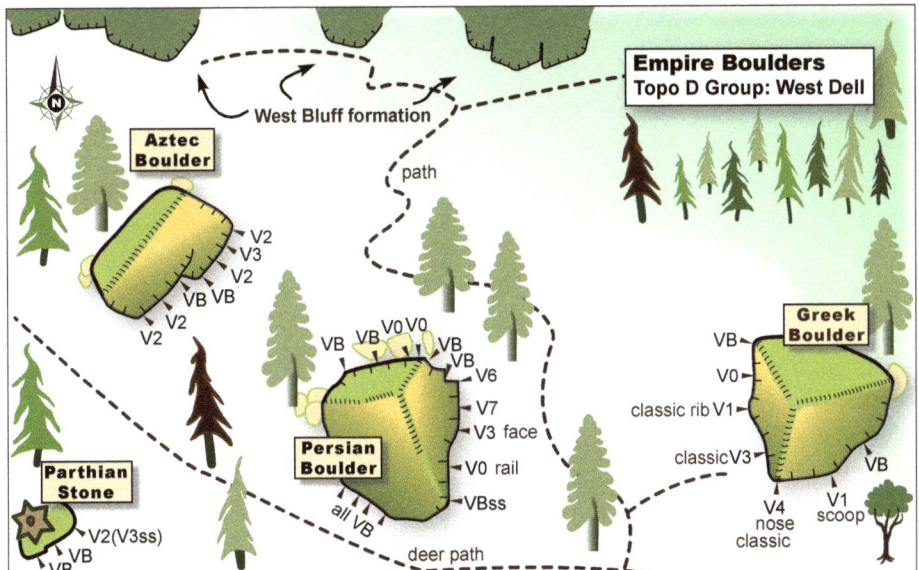

rounded nose. The classic line on this boulder.

VB Trampling March of Power ☐
Minor move; it starts at the slot but use left face only.

And...on another small stone which is on the south side of the big boulder:

V1ss Mr Cool ★★★★ ☐
Fun hung warmup arête. Just sit start low cruising a series of incut jugs up leftward onto the fun arête.

VB Paris ☐
Short slab on east face of main boulder.

Scythian Boulder

About 20' directly north uphill from the Napoleon Boulders is this small boulder.

V0ss Agnostic Babble ☐
The left mantle at the round hung nose.

V0ss Pagan Idol ☐
The right mantle just right of nose.

UPPER WEST CLUSTER

From the Rome Boulder a path extends uphill westward to a low dell or trough, where you will encounter three large boulders. The west cliff formation outcrops perch above this minor dell like little political sentinels glaring down at your slow progress. The narrower tall east-most proud stone is the Greek Stone.

Persian Boulder

This giant boulder has an excellent vertical east face with superb quality problems. The north aspect has some quality fun runs. Beta is left to right:

VB Boar's Head ☐
A minor short crimps mantle on left.

V0 Silk Road ★★★★ ☐
A great quality fun run up a steep, slightly overhung left angling rail.

V3 Trojan Horse ★★★★ ☐
Excellent vertical crimp line on a slightly overhung portion of face.

V7 Meel Time ★★★ ☐
A tech climb which starts at a series of minute pockets in a seam, and utilizes the left trending seam for the left hand. Powerful and quality.

V6 Ante Bellum ★★★ ☐
The superb 16' tall prow with a tree close at your backside.

The following are on the north aspect of this large boulder:

VB Idle Dreams ☐
The sloped corner steps.

VB Masters & Slaves ☐

Off the top of the smaller block gets one move onto slab.

V0 Rattling Sabers ★★★ ☐
Quality line that starts low in an trough between two stones. Climb a slightly hung scoop, and transition onto flat right face at mid-height, catch top lip, and mantle out. A minor variant runs left out of the scoop.

V0 Laka Educayshun ★★ ☐
Start same as previous line and transcends up right to a large pocket (crossing over next line) and continues on face up rightward to top of stone.

VB All Hat 'n No Cowboy ☐
Step off the top of the large flat block into a large foot pocket, then pull onto the top lip.

VB Genie ★ ☐
A minor steep face with a variety of crimps and edges make a nice fun run. Last problem on the uttermost northwest side.

...and on the south aspect of Persian Boulder is some family friendly short slab stuff.

VB Diva ☐
The left subtle nose onto a low angle slab.

VB Doubledip ☐
The scoop then onto the low angle slab.

VB High Five ☐
The seam smear then onto the low slab.

VB Deep-Six ☐
The bulge smear landing on the

Empire Boulders — Persian stone

Empire Boulders — Greek stone

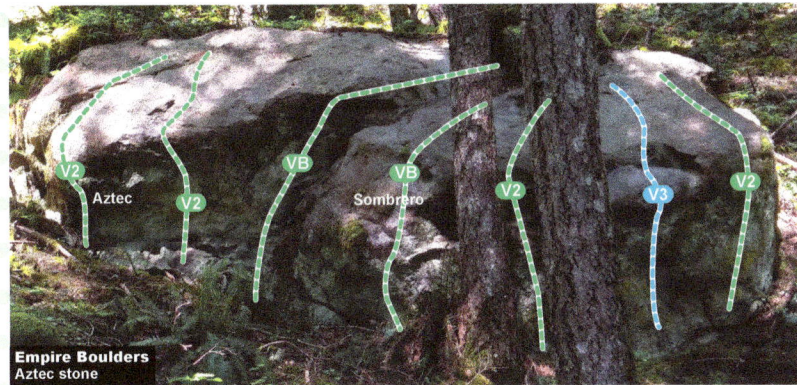

Empire Boulders
Aztec stone

low slab.

Greek Boulder

This is an excellent 15' tall stone in the upper west dell. It offers a solid string of high quality problems always worth doing. Beta is left to right:

VB Mossophobia
The down climb on the far left.

V0 Croton ★
Thin face crimps with a reachy move.

V1 Imperial Ambition ★★★★
Super classic line. Start low in center and cruise up a minor rib using various angled crimps and small edges (15' tall). Its tall.

V3 Alexander the Great ★★★★
Utilize three finger pockets to start up a vertical face. Ultra-classic line. Definitely tall but not hi-ball.

V4 Zeus ★★★★
Powerful line that starts on two pinches (left & right) and moves up into a scoop aiming for the obvious fin up high on the prow. A tech classic not to be missed.

V1 Gatekeepers ★★
Scoop-seam, mantle onto sloped slab to finish.

VB Drunk on War
Brief set of minor edges on far right.

Aztec Boulder

About 35' west of the double hitter boulders in the low dell is this last sole remain-

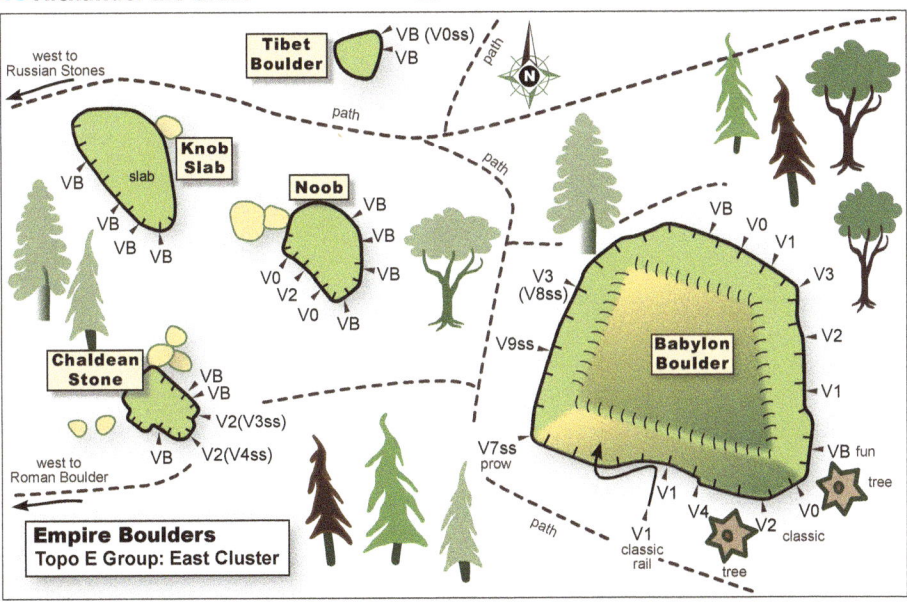

Empire Boulders
Topo E Group: East Cluster

ing challenger, a squat unit with a nice spat of brief lines on it. Beta is left to right:

V2 Aztec ★ ☐
Leftmost mantle problem onto a slab.

V2 Beast ★ ☐
Mantle a bulge onto a low angled slab.

VB Fault Line ☐
Grab rounded hung prominence and move up obvious crack rightward.

VB Sombrero ☐
Just right of the same crack, slither up onto slab (its just left of a tree).

V2 Total Depravity ★ ☐
Right side of tree at hollow flake. Punch over round bulge onto slab.

V3 Utopian Visionaire ★ ☐
Crimps on rounded bulge reaching for a pocket on a slab.

V2 Sanity Awakening ☐
Use crimps on rounded bulge on far right.

LOWER EAST CLUSTER

In the east cluster are three massive boulders with a broad variety of high quality lines. Many must-do lines exist on the Babylon, Inca and Spanish Boulder. A prominent trail goes directly east from Roman Boulder to Babylon Boulder.

Babylon Boulder

This is a very massive stone, and a fine spectrum of quality lines await for those who like lower spectrum grades. Beta is clockwise starting on the north side. The problems on the south aspect are definitely tall, nearly hi-ball.

VB Ur ★★★ ☐

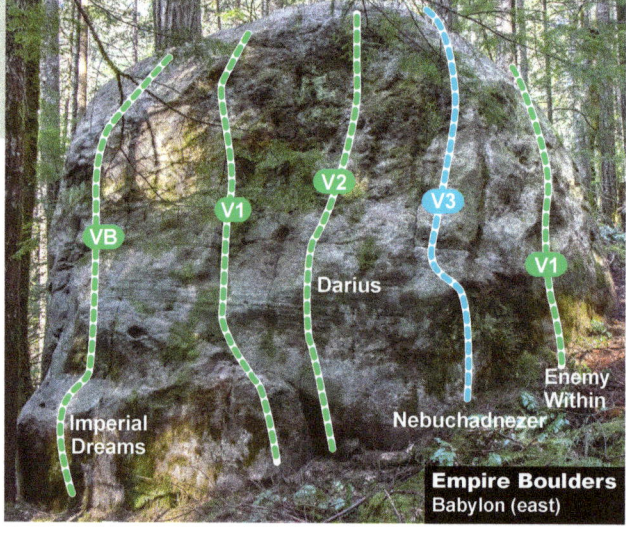

Babylon Boulder • GB 73

Empire Boulders
Babylon (south)

A fun quality short string of pockets leading up to a slight round dish.

V0 Graveyard of Empires ★★★★ ☐
Obvious string of small pockets ending with sloper crimps. A minor variation exists between this and the previous.

V1 Enemy Within ★★★ ☐
Several nice jugs to start, then ends with a few skinny crimps. Cool spook.

V3 Nebuchadnezer ★★★★ ☐

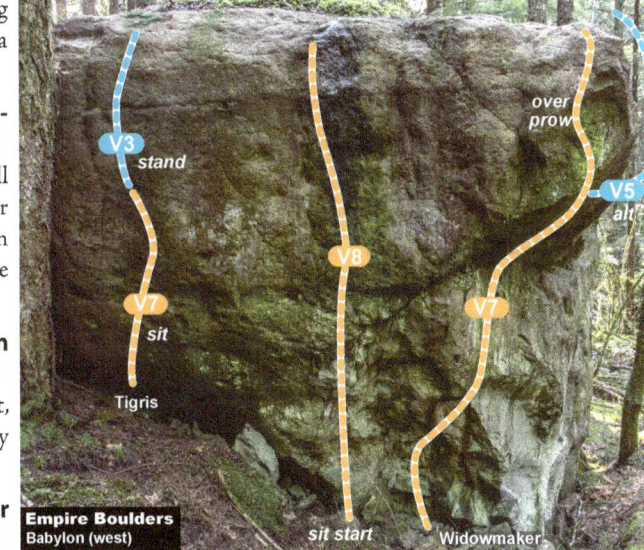

Empire Boulders
Babylon (west)

Start up a seam, smearing and crimps will get you a fair high hold, then a series of tricky thin crimps (crux) at the top give you a quality tall finale.

V2 Darius ★★★ ☐
Initial starter move, and crux cross-over gets you into the slight groove to several nice pockets, then ends with a flat topped finale.

V1 Xerxes ★ ☐
Initial step move, then steepens to vertical dicey thin face crux at the top.

VB Imperial Dreams ★★★★ ☐
Start on the immediate right side of the large fir tree, grab a large obvious pocket, and dash up the easy terrain to a brief vertical crux move. Fun tall climb.

V0 Tower of Babel ★★★ ☐
Start on the immediate left side of a large tree, and dance up numerous holds. Where it steepens, a series of large pockets await with a minor crux move. Fun tall problem. Located between the two fir trees. Excellent problem.

V2 Seventh Wonder ★★★★ ☐
A superb very tall problem on a vertical face with several big pockets on its upper portion. Located between the two trees. This is the left of two cool side by side routes. Classic!

V4 Fiery Furnace ★ ☐
A right angling corner-ish seam, that gets vertical and very dicey at the last portion of the problem. Crux is the very last move.

V1 Spice & Dice ★ ☐
Start low in center of face (same as for next line), move up left a few moves along the rail system, then punch straight up using a series of small crimps on a vertical face. Better holds save you at the exit.

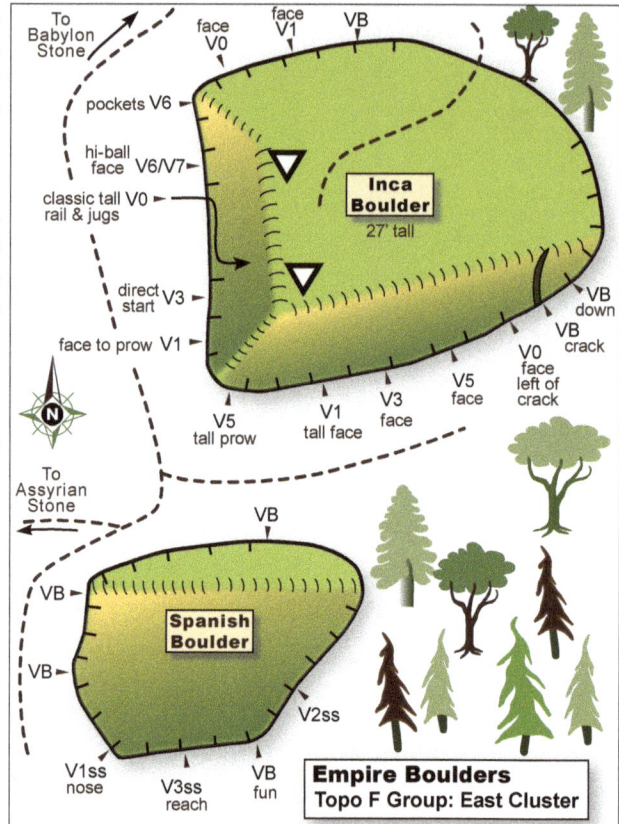

Tymun on *Native Soul*

Babylon Boulder • GB 75

Empire Boulders — Inca stone

V1 The Emperor ★★★★
A cool line at EB. Start low in the center of south face aspect. Run the rail monkey style leftward, then as a high bulge of rock begins to jut out, crimp directly up the slightly overhung face on crux small holds.

V7ss Widowmaker ★★★
The powerful reachy super overhung west prow. Another (V7) variant is to run the classic rail leftward into this super overhung prow problem.

V8ss Enemy (at the gates)
Thin rounded pockets and scoops on short overhung face.

V3 (V7ss) Tigris ★★
Next to the tree trunk is a brief power move with a sloped top out.

Inca Boulder

This is the tallest tumbled boulder at Empire, logging in at a wildly majestic 27' tall on its west aspect. The beta begins on its north side (Left to Right), ending on its south side:

VB Stone Stairs
Basic steps on far left (north side).

V1 Native Soul ★★★
Quality enjoyable short sequence of moves using two small crimp slopers.

V0 At The Table Or On The Menu ★★
A tall rounded face with series of angled seam-edges for crimps and smears (very close to a fir tree). Fine quality line.

V6 Pyramid ★★★ ⚠
Tall techy face with pockets and knobs ending on an arête on upper portion.

V7 High Priestess ★ ⚠

Tall face (start same as next) that goes up through a slightly hung scoop to a high crux, then exits left (direct finish is harder at V7/8).

V0 Machu Pichu ★★★★

Premier central route on the tall west face. Crux opening move to jugs, and crux exit move. Great hi-ball problem.

V3 Directissimo

Vertical direct that merges into previous route.

V1 Imperial Hubris ★★

Vertical face with nice pockets; merges onto arête at mid-height to finish.

V5 Blood Sacrifice ★★★

Long arête with low crimps crux, then from mid stance upward are easier rounded reachy holds.

V1 Pulmonary Edema ★★★★

Superb classic route on the tall south face. Go up arched seam, then up steep slab on better holds.

V3 Manco Capac ★★★

Crux opening move is a single small inclusion, then continue on small holds on a tall face. Excellent route.

V6 Bleeding Edge ★★★

Superb techy line. Thin opening moves to a slight hung rounded lip. Dicey crux slopers above lip.

V0 Nowhere Fast ★★★

Start of small holds on left

Empire Boulders
Inca (south)

Empire Boulders
Spanish

side of crack system (rules left of crack for all holds). At stance make a crux move to small pocket up right.

VB Ibex
The fat curved OW crack system.

VB Fen Fu
Far right down step.

Spanish Boulder

Just a few yards to the south of the Inca Boulder is the Spanish Boulder. Though squat-like with a broad slab top-out, the south aspect does offer several nice lines. Beta is left to right:

VB Hobgoblin
Minor slab seam on the north side.

VB Spaniard
Round slabby west ramp.

VB Galleon
Minor scoop and slab on west side.

V1 Columbus ★
The bulge at a round nose (onto slab).

V3ss Doobloon ★★
A bulge with a scoop that refutes the less than diligent. On south aspect of stone.

VB Realm of Uncertainty ★★
Vertical fun run using positive holds on center of the south aspect of stone.

V2 Mandolin ★
A nice string of moves that makes a high step onto the slab finish.

Assyrian Boulder

About 50' directly west of the Spanish Boulder is this extremely low obscure flat stone. Beta is from left to right.

V2ss Blackball ★★
Left low bulge (rules: avoid seam).

V0ss Unthinkable Thinkster ★★
Up just the seam (rules: seam only). Low start.

VB Imperial Umpires
Mere high step one move.

V0ss Fastball
Low start using several incut small pockets (rules: just the pockets).

Empire Boulders
Chaldean

The next three minor boulders (Knob, Noob, Chaldean) are located in a cluster just west of the Babylon Boulder about 35' distance.

Knob Slab

A fun low angle 12' slab with a liberal dose of knobs, located next to the main east-west deer path. No photo, but very kids quality.

VB Pork Bellies ★★
All four problems on Knob Slab (5.0-5.3).

Noob Boulder

An inconsequential argumentative uncooperative tiny stone. No photo.

V0 Noob. Squnched tightly left of the next unit.

V2 Motherland pockets (left-right), high step right, top slopers.

V0 Fatherland the high step south side.

VB All Noob. South and east side ramps, and two short kids east side lines.

Chaldean Boulder

Directly west of Babylon Stone about 30' is this stone with a brief 'ss' overhang. Beta is from right to left:

VBss Noob
Squnchable kids line on right.

VB (V1ss) Just Do It
Short crimps line.

V2 (**V3ss**) **Whiskey & Whine** ★ ☐

Start on right side, latch rounded nose, get up.

V2 (**V4ss**) **Crocodile Tears** ★ ☐

Start low on two finger slopers, left foot way out left, launch to fix on bulge jug, get up over.

Hittite Boulder

Minor stone between Chaldean and Scythian stones. Both problems are very short.

VB Schmoo ☐

VB Whangdoodle ☐

Tibet Boulder

A very minor small roundish stone just northeast of Knob Slab on the path en route to the Han Face (on the bluff outcrop).

VB (**V0ss**) **Broken Spear** ☐
Standing jug mantle, or sit start on crimps below jug.

VB War 'n Peace ☐
A one move smear left of the previous line.

Byzantine Boulder

Just north of the Babylon Boulder, walk the deer path for 80' to this minor 10' tall stone. The south side is flat faced and offers four brief odd lines.

VB Iconoclast ☐
The left nose for a few moves.

VB Byzantine ★ ☐
Run the lip uphill from Left to Right ending high on rightmost VB.

VB Tetragram ☐
Midway one move step-in.

VB Constantinople ☐
Direct dance on the taller portion (rules out any big foot hold).

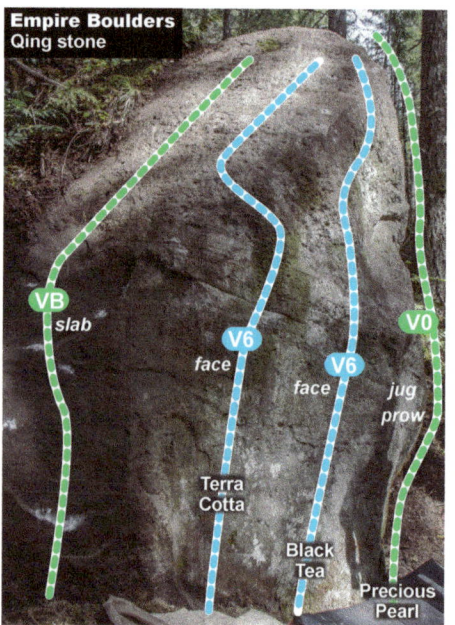

Byzantine Boulder • GB 79

GREAT WALL OF CHINA

This refers to the bluff outcrops that protrude from a steep hillside. The Great Wall offers an exhilerating and extensive selection of serious hi-ball lines, some classic lines, and possibly even the stoutest mega overhung face at the Empire Boulders. These various outcrops are given a Chinese dynastic reference name to parallel the major dynasties.

Each of the outcrops are described from right to left (beginning at the far east end at the Yuan stone and culminating at the far west end of the outcrop bluff formation beyond the Japan stone).

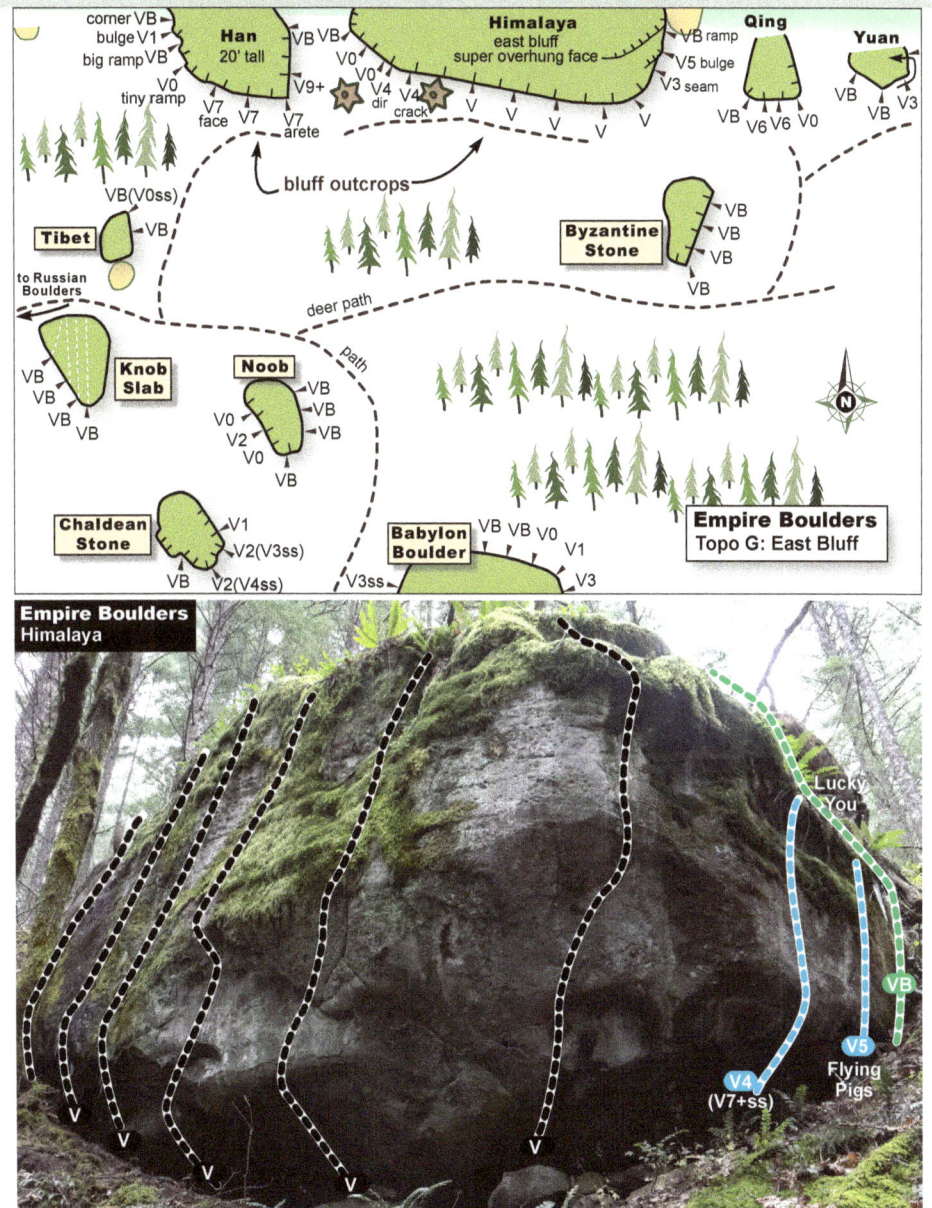

Yuan Dynasty

At the utter east end of the outcrops (beyond even the Qing) is a tipsy little speck of stone. This is the Yuan Stone with a very minor set of lines. Beta is left to right:

VBss Bondage ☐
Left side low 'ss', then mantle over.

VBss Between Good & Evil ☐
Start at pockets on center point, mantle over.

Empire Boulders
Himalaya (left)

V3ss Enemy of Your Enemy ★★★ ☐
Just right of previous, run right horizontally around the hung prow, and mantle over far right side. Quality problem.

V0ss Gutless Wonder ☐
Mantle the far east side.

And another 150' further to the east is a VB minor on an isolated tiny munch block.

Qing Dynasty Boulder

Qing-Manchu is the second small outcrop along the cliffband. Beta is right to left:

V0 Precious Pearl ★★★★ ☐
Quality vertical layback rib with opening crux move (rules avoid big flat stance part way up on right).

V6 Black Tea ★★★ ☐
Powerful and thin. Right sidepull crimp, send middle part of face via left sloped crest.

V5 Terra Cotta ★★ ☐
Start on obvious fat flat hold on left, go up to small divots high on left face.

VB Polished Jade ★ ☐
Easy slab on the left side of stone.

Himalaya Face ⚠

Incredible super overhung face about 25' tall at its center. It offers about 5 futuristic hi-ball potential problems, some pushing the edge (V10-12+). Beta is Right to Left (east

Himalaya Face • GB 81

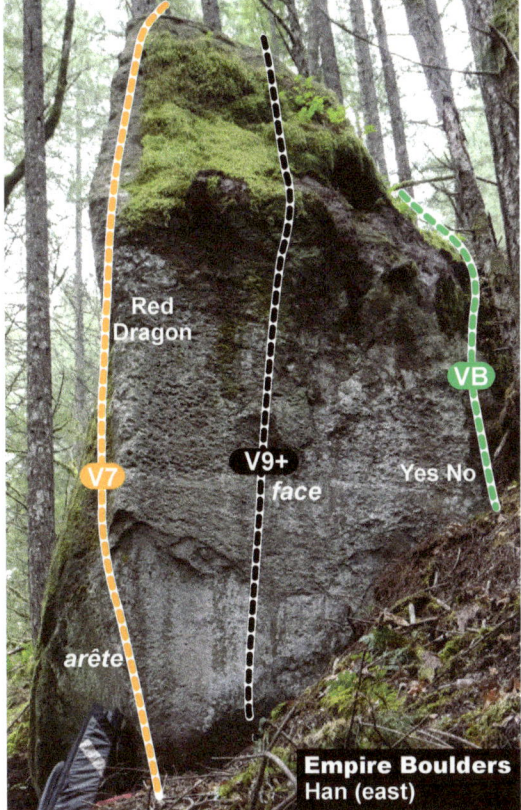

to west).

VB Lucky You ★
Basic rightmost low-angle ramp.

V5 Flying Pigs ★
Brief bulge mantle onto slab.

V4 (V7ss+) Divine Fury
Crimps at a seam. Powerful sit start under entire formation.

V_ (?) ___ ⚠
The super hung face.

V_ (?) ___ ⚠
The super hung face.

V_ (?) ___ ⚠
The super hung face.

V_ (?) ___ ⚠
The super hung face.

V_ (?) ___ ⚠
The super hung face.

V4 The Sword ★ ⚠
Tall cool thin finger crack (p).

V4 Unreal Unperson ★★
Direct using smears and long reach to two pockets, then finish on seam.

V0 Logic ★★
Brief smear and crimps on rightward angling seam.

V0ss Szechuan ★★★
Crimp reach, pull to a crimp, attain top lip, mantle, done.

VB Manchu ★
Leftmost fun basic nose.

Han Dynasty Boulder ⚠

Prominent bluff with two main aspects with impressive 25' sharp arête. Beta is right to left:

VB Yes No Maybe ★
Basic groove next to a tree (on east side).

V8+ (?) ___ ⚠
The vertical crimps east face; the higher line.

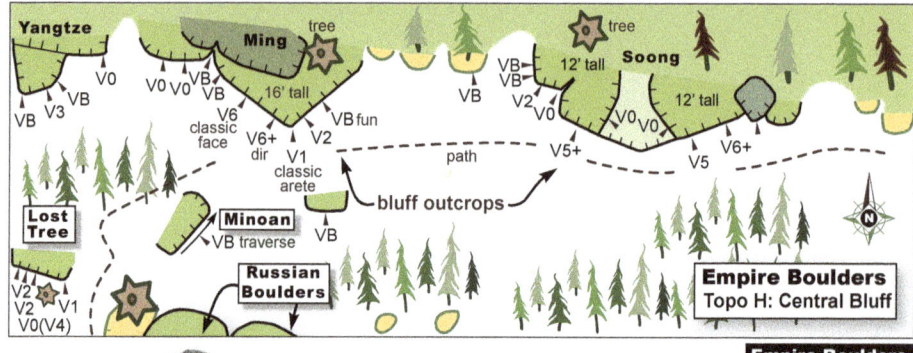

Empire Boulders — Topo H: Central Bluff

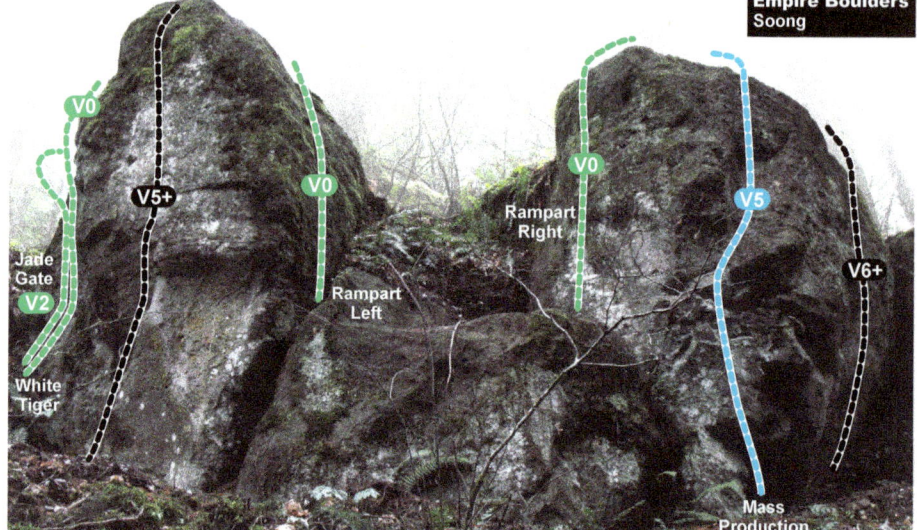

Empire Boulders — Soong

V9+ (?)
Vertical powerful thin crimps on east face.

V7 Red Dragon ★★★★
The ultra classic arête and one of the great reasons to be here. Begin directly below arête on right side, then transition up onto its left side, while using right hand on arête to top.

V7 Automation ★★★
Delicate face crimps to mid-stance, then techy moves up vertical face. Excellent line.

V7 The Empress ★★★
Thin crimps, crux onto sloped stance, then crux exit at top lip. Stellar line.

VB (V0ss) Jade ★★★★
Right angled tiny ramp [landing #3] to a block pinch, then high step up left into the crack corner system (the next VB). The V0 variant starts on second landing. V3 is the direct fin-

ish. A variant exists starting on the lowest landing crossing up into this line.

VB Shanghai ★★★ ⚠
Fun hi-ball corner with large pockets, crack-ish nuance, and bulge at the top.

V1 Loaded Dice ★
Up easy steps to a right hand pocket, then power over a short bulge onto top.

VB Cobwebs
Very short round groove corner.

Soong Boulder

A unique double-set of overhung outcrops with a flat ledge squnched between each outcrop. Several quality lines exist on both. Beta is right to left (starting at the east outcrop):

V6-9 (?) ___
The super hung crimps east face (project).

V5 Mass Production ★★★
Great opening jugs to start and powerful crimps to finish.

V0 Rampart Right
Short face starting off a high landing.

...and on the west part of this outcrop:

V0 Rampart Left
The other short face off a high flat landing.

V5+ (?) Mirabile Visu
Powerful hung techy crimp-*fest* (project).

V0 White Tiger ★★
Quality short hung crack.

V2 Jade Gate ★★★
Quality crimps. Start at the V0 crack, go up left face to next VB.

VB & VB (one move problems). VB rounder stone (to the left about 15').

Ming Boulder

Just uphill northward about 30' from the Russian Boulders is this tall 17' high outcrop

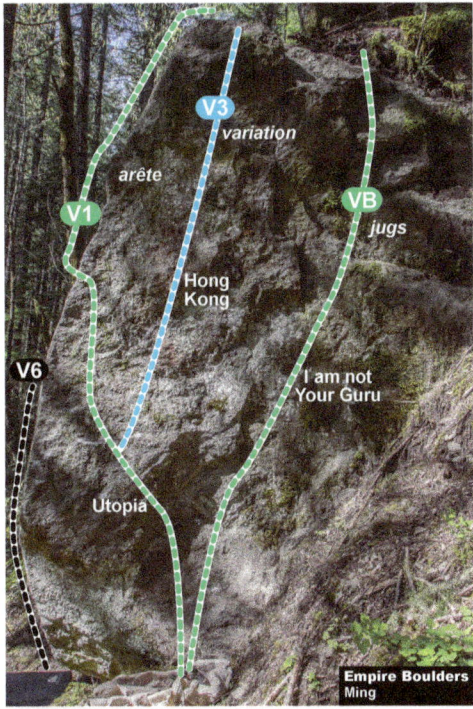
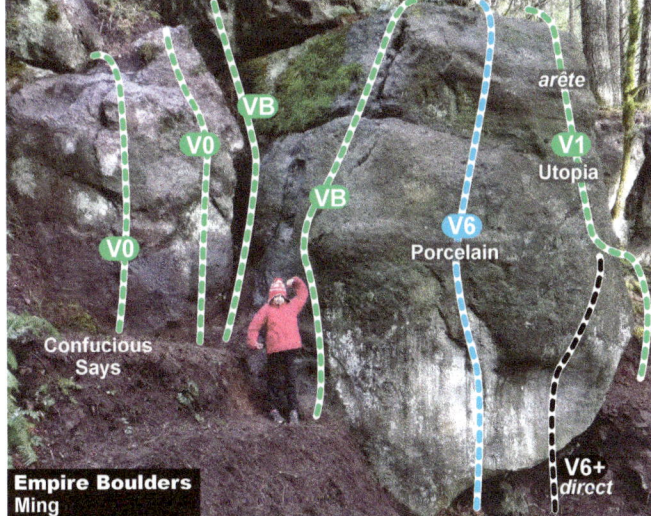

with numerous stellar lines. Beta is from right to left:

VB I Am Not Your Guru ★★★★
Cruise up incut sidepulls and slopers on vertical face (right side of outcrop). The *first* boulder problem established on the bluff outcrops.

V2 Hong Kong ★
Stay on the right side of arête all the way (left

84 EMPIRE BOULDERS • Ming Boulder

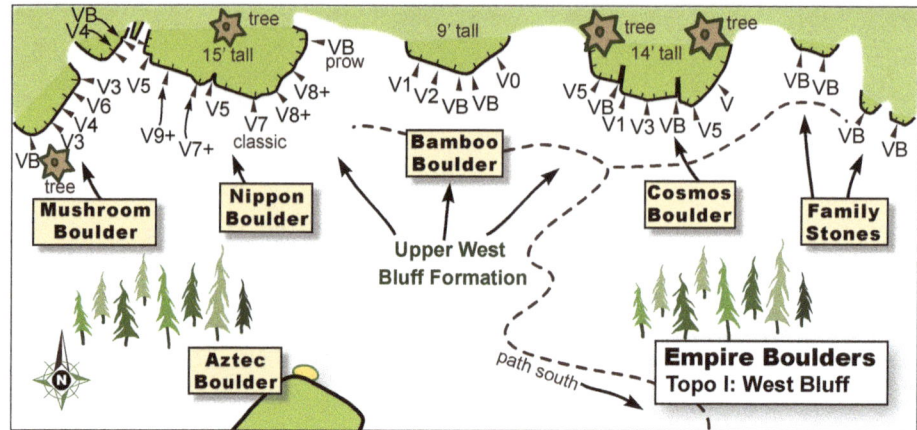

hand on arête).

V1 Utopia ★★★★ ⚠
Classic arête. Cruise up east side, transfer to the arêtes left side at tiny mid-height stance, then dicey crux move to top. Exit left before crux is V0.

V6-7 (?) Mittimus ★ ⚠
Hung scoop face that merges into the upper arête of previous line (p).

V6 Porcelain ★★★★ ⚠
Ultra classic face and serious hi-ball. Begin in a slight overhung scoop and utilize tiny pockets, small knobs and slopers. Way to go Mr A!

VB Royal Blood ★★★
On left side of stone. Basic curved seams and edges (good fun run).

VB Huckypuk
The fat dirty offwidth.

V0 Fuzzy Thinking ★★
Crimpy cool face immediately left of the OW.

V0 Confucious Says ★★
A short crimp seam on a short face.

Yangtze Boulder

Paul on *Gladiator*

A low angle slab with a midway landing, then a brief vertical second tier (kind of like a multi-pitch climb). Just uphill from Lone Tree Boulder. Beta is from left to right:

VB WhoWhatWhy ❏
A basic initial crux smear move, then a slab run. Step right at dirt landing to tackle a V0 finalé on the next shorty tier.

V3 Dirt Bag ❏
Start low on right at odd crimp maneuver.

VB Boorish Crack ❏
No cookies; crack to slab.

UPPER WEST BLUFF

In the upper west dell (about 40' above the Greek, Persian and Aztec Boulders) is a series of bluff outcrops. These outcrops yield a variety of fun runs, packed with plenty of ultra powerful lines that are the real deal.

Family Boulders

Three very tiny stones with a few basic brief VB's for kids to dash up all located to the east of the next boulder.

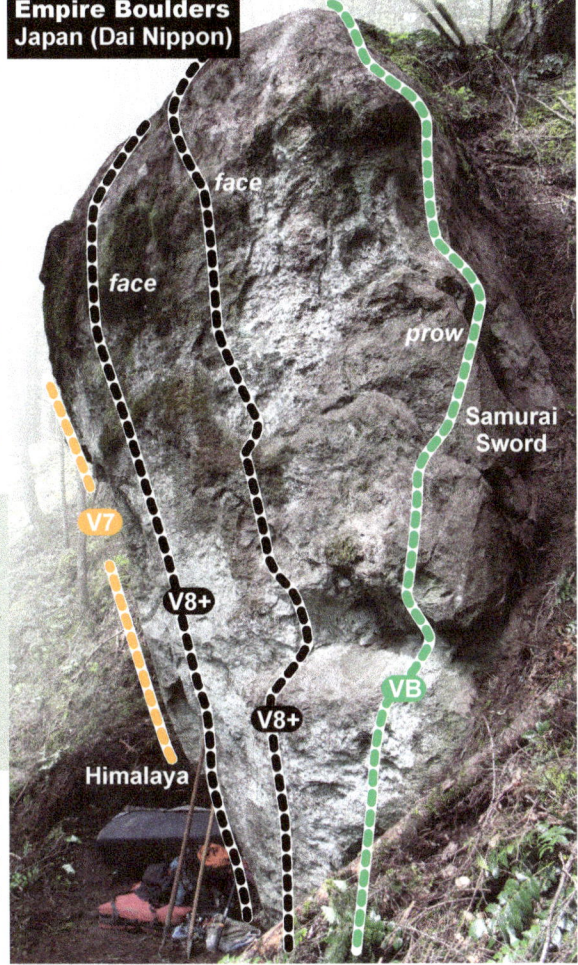

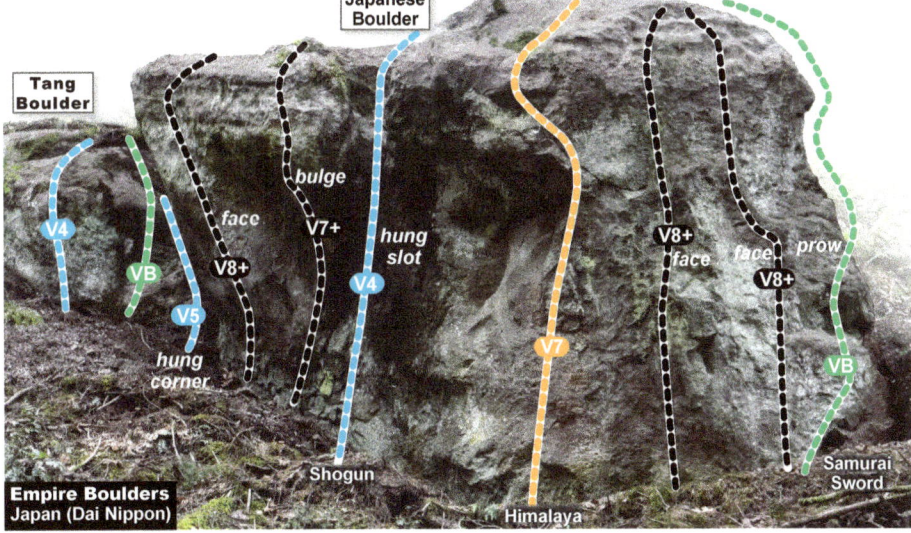

Cosmos Boulder

A fairly tall (14' high) outcrop with a vertical east prow. Beta is listed right to left:

V8+ (?) ___
Futuristic right face crimps.

V6 Globalism ★★
Powerful crimps on tall jutting overhung arête (p).

VB Shenanigans
Wide corner crack system on the right.

V3ss Copore Sano ★★
The sit start begins below jug, power over bulge, chill at stance, then finesse over the top lip.

V1ss Propaganda ★★★
Low sit start Nice hung minor arête (the right side of OW) with crimps to a stance, then pull over the top lip on crimps.

VB Cosmos ★
The left big fat OW crack.

V5ss The One ★★★★
Tricky initial setup and powerful crimps on this fine quality face line.

Bamboo Boulder

Midway between the two major stones is this minor shorty stone. Beta is right to left.

V0ss Far East
Low minor one-move-two.

VB Nine Yak Tails
Outer crack one move wonder.

VB Bamboo
Left start on face ending in crack.

V2ss Kim Chi ★
Just 'ss' low on crimpy short face.

V1ss Serpent ★
Just 'ss' low on short crimpy face.

Japanese Boulder ⚠

Dai Nippon (the Japanese Boulder). Impressive 17' tall outcrop with a serious overhang, and a fine string of ultra-wild lines. The

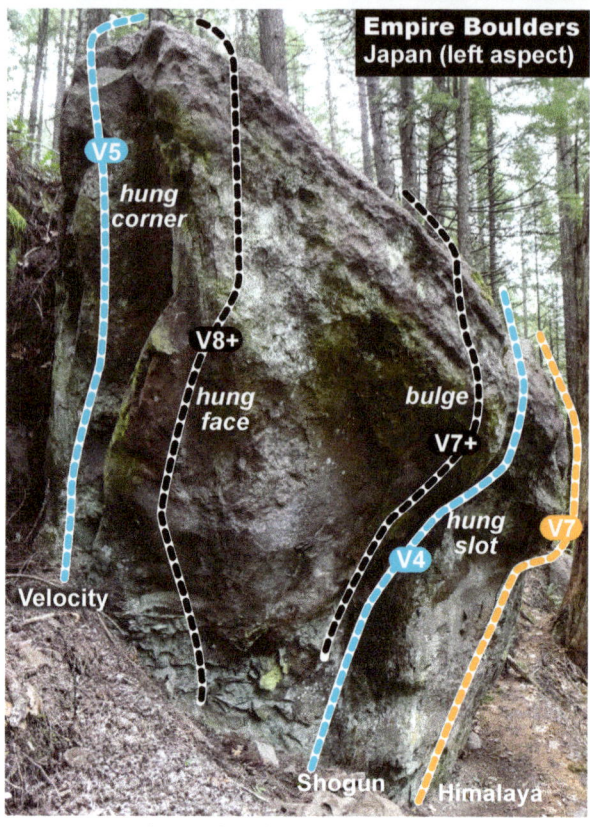

Empire Boulders Japan (left aspect)

beta is listed right to left:

VB Samurai Sword ★★★ ⚠
Stellar warmup route using crimps on the hiball east prow. Always worth doing. Crux is the last move.

V8+ Yamamoto ⚠
Flat crimps face on right aspect (starts powerful, then gets more so). Project.

V8+ Fuji ⚠
Start on jugs, quickly morph to extreme sloper crimps (project).

V7 Himalaya ★★★★ ⚠
Classic powerful hung prow just right of fat slot. Power flat crimps to hung lip, trend up left then over top bulge.

V5 Shogun ★ ⚠
Overhung fat slot full on.

V7+ Rising Sun ⚠
The jutting overhung bulge just left of the fat slot (project).

V8+ss Real Mojo ⚠
Technical hung crimps face (left hand uses edge of dihedral) (project).

V5 Velocity ★★★★
Far west overhung short dihedral corner involving unique crimps and moves. Classic, deceptive, powerful. Superb problem.

Tang Boulder

VB Intellectual Idiots
Minor short seam (rightmost line).

V4 Emperor's Clothes
Crimps over bulge.

Mushroom Boulder

The final westmost bluff outcrop at Empire. A shorty 9' tall stone, with a few punchy odd minor problems. Cheers to the mushroom man! Beta is listed right to left.

V2 (V3ss) Forest Frenzy
Minor round short face on the right.

V6 Spore ★
Power crimps on short face ending on slab.

V4 Express ★
Flat short crimps face ending on slab.

V3 Panda Bear ★★★
Make a move, catch the nob, reposition balance, mantle slowly. Phew!

VBss Chantrelle ★
Ultra shorty on far left.

Parthian Boulder

A tiny tiny isolated stone located about 100' southwest of the Persian/Aztec boulders. Beta is listed right to left.

V2 (V3ss) Square Peg Round Hole
Crimp rounded shorty rounded nose.

VBss Red Herring
Center shorty line.

VBss Zero
Leftmost shorty line.

And at that final tiny boulder we wrap up the entire discussion about the Empire Boulders. So how's that for a power packed group of boulder problems (VB to V-insane), all of it stacked majestically into one single impressive bouldering zone that close to Portland, Oregon?

Totally cool....

Empire Boulders Mushroom

Sunny Eastside Bouldering

1

HORSETHIEF BUTTE

The popular Horsethief Butte offers an ideal respite from the liberal amounts of western Oregon rain where you can often find sunny weather crag climbing by the Columbia River.

For rock climbers it offers a tremendous variety of short boulder problems within a series of corridors in the inner portion of the butte. This site offers an effective means to practice and enhance the basic concepts of rock climbing and rappeling. The natural open atmosphere of the inner butte offers easy communication from instructor to climber.

BRIEF HISTORY OF THE AREA

The Butte is a prominent feature within the Columbia Hills State Park and is a popular site for climbing as well as hiking. The nearby lake was formed when The Dalles Dam was built.

For centuries local American Indians lived near the Butte. The ease of access to the river also provided excellent opportunity for them to catch some of the seasonal migration of salmon for food and for barter. Celilo Falls was the heart of a long established trading region that sustained a thriving community of native Indians from the Wisham, Cloud and Lishkam tribes. The Lewis and Clark expedition camped at a village during their journey west in 1805-1806. Salmon caught near the Celilo Falls provided an important source for trade and barter with other indigenous native tribes of the region. Excellent remnants of native Indian petroglyphs such as *she who watches* provide visitors with archeological insight of ancient tribal customs.

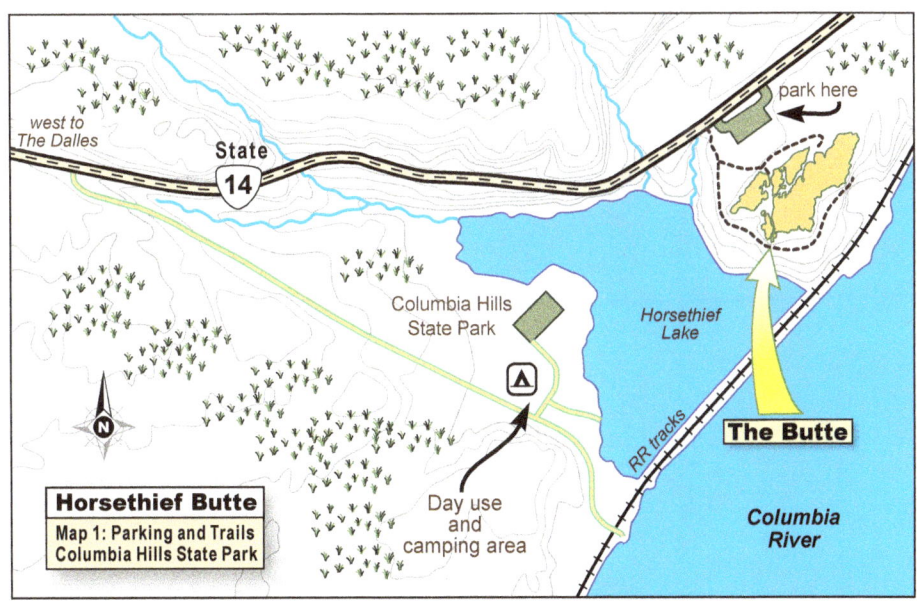

VISITOR CONSIDERATIONS AND STATE PARK REGULATIONS

- Horsethief Butte has several areas signed as 'no climbing' for cultural resource protection. Columbia Hills State Park has archeological sites including Horsethief Butte which are protected by State and Federal laws. Disturbance and/or removal of any artifact, pictograph, or petroglyph is prohibited.
- Expect windy conditions.
- Beware of the occasional rattlesnake. Frequent visitor foot traffic tends to keep most rattlesnakes at a distance.
- Poison Oak grows along the base of several walls. This thick short shrub has seasonal glossy leaves which grow in groups of three per branch and have small white berries.
- Ticks are common in the Spring and Fall seasons. Ticks are quite small so be certain to inspect for ticks if you visit here. There is a plethora of bouldering problems beyond what this section could possibly convey, but this in-depth treatise strives to detail the greater portion of the well traveled climbs found at the Butte.

Most of the beta within this particular section includes dual grades. First is the bouldering V-scale grade, listed as if you are going to treat the problem as a bouldering event. Somewhere in the description is the standard YDS grade for various problems that are in the hi-ball range. Many problems here are hi-ball. A few routes are generally only viable as top-rope or lead routes. Many of the problems here have at one time or another been solo bouldered (even though many do have substantial height risk issues). Horsethief Butte is ideal for, and often utilized for, both types (bouldering or climbing) of recreation activity. For the boulderer it's a nice all-year place to carefully learn some hi-ball technique on often easy climbing terrain. Just beware that certain landings need well padded.

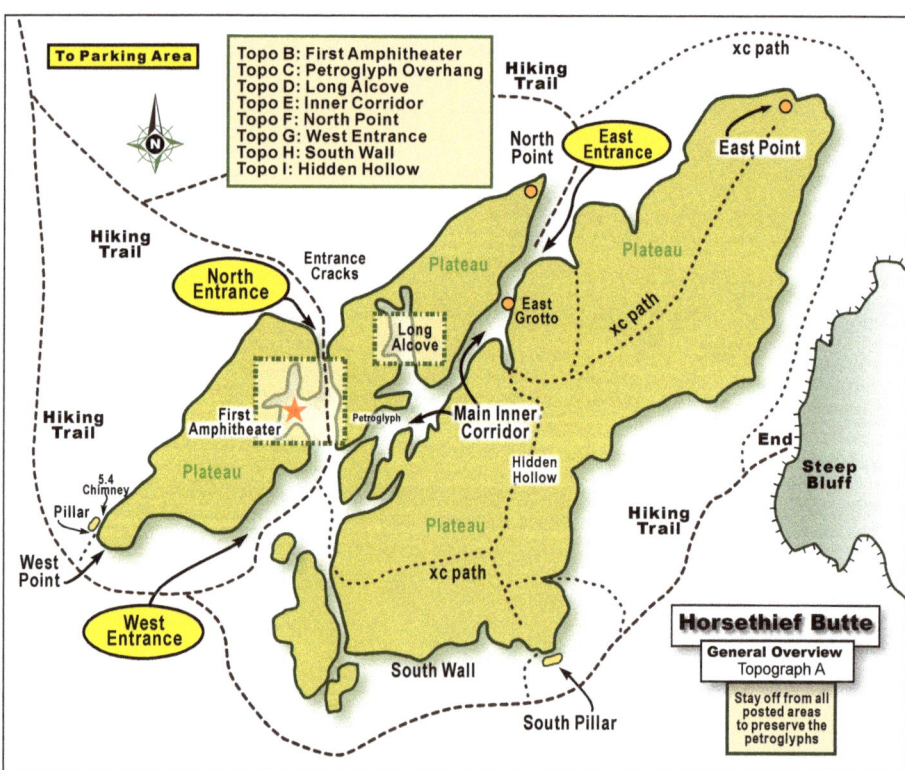

DIRECTIONS

Directions from Oregon: From exit #87 at The Dalles drive north across the Columbia River bridge on U.S. 197 for 3½ miles, then east on Washington State 14 for 2¾ miles to Columbia Hills State Park. The Butte is located east of the lake at Mile Post 85. Park along the highway shoulder immediately across a small bridge. Hike on the path south to the butte and enter either via the west side trail or at the 'Entrance Cracks' gap in the wall. Camping (closed from Nov. thru March) is available at the developed facility on the west side of the 90-acre Horsethief lake. Climb safely and enjoy your visit!

Entrance Cracks ⚠

Always popular place to climb, but generally a bit too hi-ball for bouldering. The entry cracks corridor is the common way to enter into the main inner zones at the Butte, and you will pass by these fine looking tall crack routes en route to your bouldering projects.

1. VB OW & Hand Crack ★★
Left of the left prow are several climbs in the shaded portion of the bluff. Both begin up the same crack using edges and steps. From the midway stance, embark up *left* in a wide offwidth crack using a small hidden edge in the offwidth which leads to better edges at the top (rated about 5.8). The *right* jam crack is closer to the arête (rated 5.9). Ascend the lower crack to the midway stance, then embark up right into a jam crack which forces you to use the arête more than the crack. There are several more thin optional climbs just to the left of these two climbs that are fairly difficult.

2. VB Jam Crack ★★
Great hand and fist jam climb (5.9). Start initially in the Left Entrance Crack and punch out left to a short vertical jam crack.

3. V1 Left Entrance Crack ★★★
This is the left major corner system (5.10+). Ascend the steep tricky corner by smearing

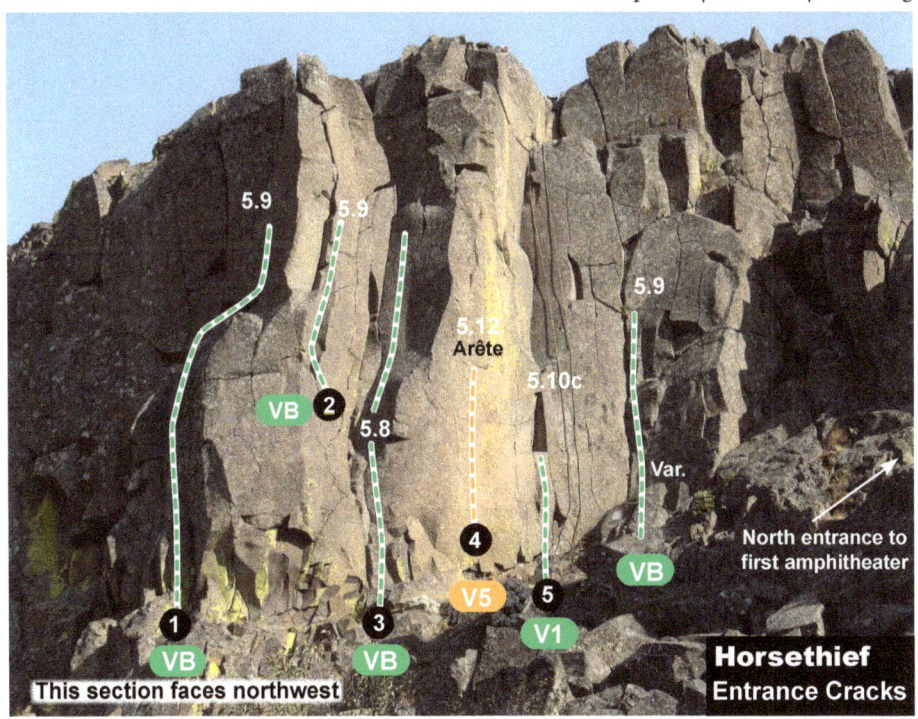

delicately on smooth sloped holds using the thin crack where possible. No such thing as a free lunch.

4. V5 Arête ☐

Between the two Entrance Crack routes is a technical minor arête top-rope (5.12).

5. V0 Right Entrance Crack ★ ★ ★ ☐

This is the right most (and best) of two classic corner systems known as the Entrance Cracks. Involves long reaches, technical smears, and powerful layback moves using a jam crack (rating 5.10-). On the right face of this entrance crack is another minor seam that branches up right at about VB (5.9) which might be bouldered (with crashpads).

The Passageway

This is the main corridor passageway you walk in passing the Entrance Cracks on your left to reach the inner bouldering zones.

These next two under-age minors are situated together on the east wall of the Passageway just as it opens into the First Amphitheater.

6. V0 Face ☐

A short smooth face ending on a ledge (5.10-).

7. V1 Arête ☐

Another short problem next to the previous

The next two steep problems are found on the west wall of the Passageway.

8. VB Corner ★ ☐

Layback up the pillar and stem the corner (5.8) onto the flat top.

9. VB Corner ★ ☐

Climb up a crack in a corner with a long reach to finish (5.7) ending on a flat top.

First Amphitheater

The following string begins on the west side of the Passageway and curls around the initial buttress counter-clockwise into the First Main Am-

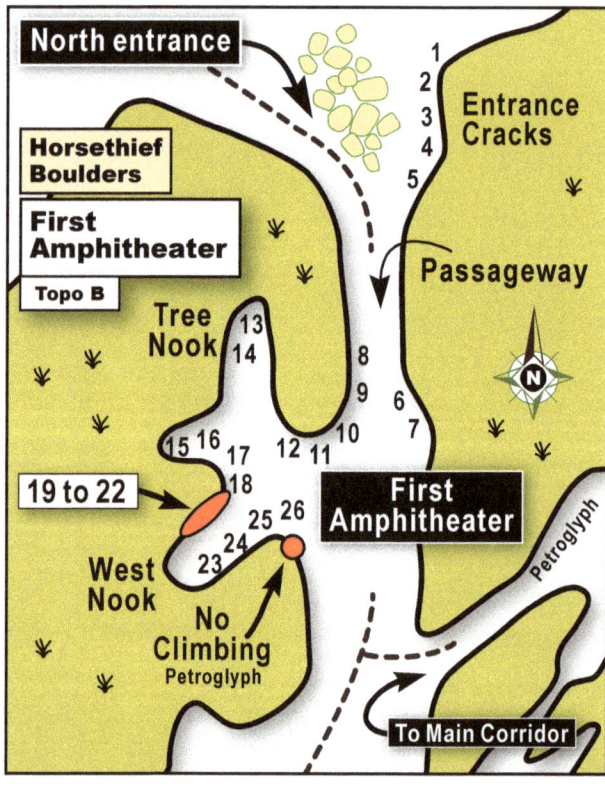

phitheater. Two nooks (north tree nook and west nook) provide a great series of problems.

Wide Buttress

10. V0 Groove
Climb the tight side of the buttress (5.10-).

11. VB Smooth Dihedral
In the middle of the buttress climb up a dihedral corner using jams and stemming (5.7).

12. V0 Discontinuous Cracks
Broken cracks on the left most side of the buttress (5.10-).

Tree Nook

This is a tiny nook with a small tree tucked in the corner.

13. VB Face ★
Deep in the Tree Nook on the left side before the small tree is a tall face. Climb up the well-featured and cracked patina face (5.9) to a tricky finish.

14. V1 Crack-Prow
In the same Tree Nook left of the tall face is a crack/prow (5.10+). You can jam or bear hug this problem.

Half Nook

15. V1 Thin Crack
A shorty problem (5.10+). Use the right diagonal crack on a smooth slab.

16. VB Green Slab
This is the outermost nose of a low angle slab.

17. V1 Prow
Climb the left side of the prow to a mantle (5.10+).

18. V1 Overhang
Start on a left trending seam (5.10c). Climb up to a jug and mantle.

West Nook - Right routes

West Nook is a stellar place to learn bouldering technique at the Butte.

West Nook also offers a great punchy thin traverse all the way to Half Nook.

19. VB Flake
A great warm up flake climb (5.8) problem.

20. V1 Crack Seam ★ ★ ★
This classic line (and the next one) are the central feature of the West Nook. They offer complexity, steepness, and quality great for bouldering (5.10+).

21. Corner V2 to V4 ★ ★ ★
Stellar V2 thin crack corner that is much harder than it looks. Using rules staying in the crack will make it V3. Traversing in from the far left then up the corner crack is V4.

22. V7 Face
Climb the thin face left of the corner using just the small holds on the face.

West Nook - Left routes

23. VB Low Angle Face
This is on the south side of the West Nook. Climb up on jug holds.

24. V0 Face
Climb up through the missing block.

25. V2 Crack System
Start on the jug and climb up the shallow crack to a flake.

Jerad on a V4, the *Narrows*

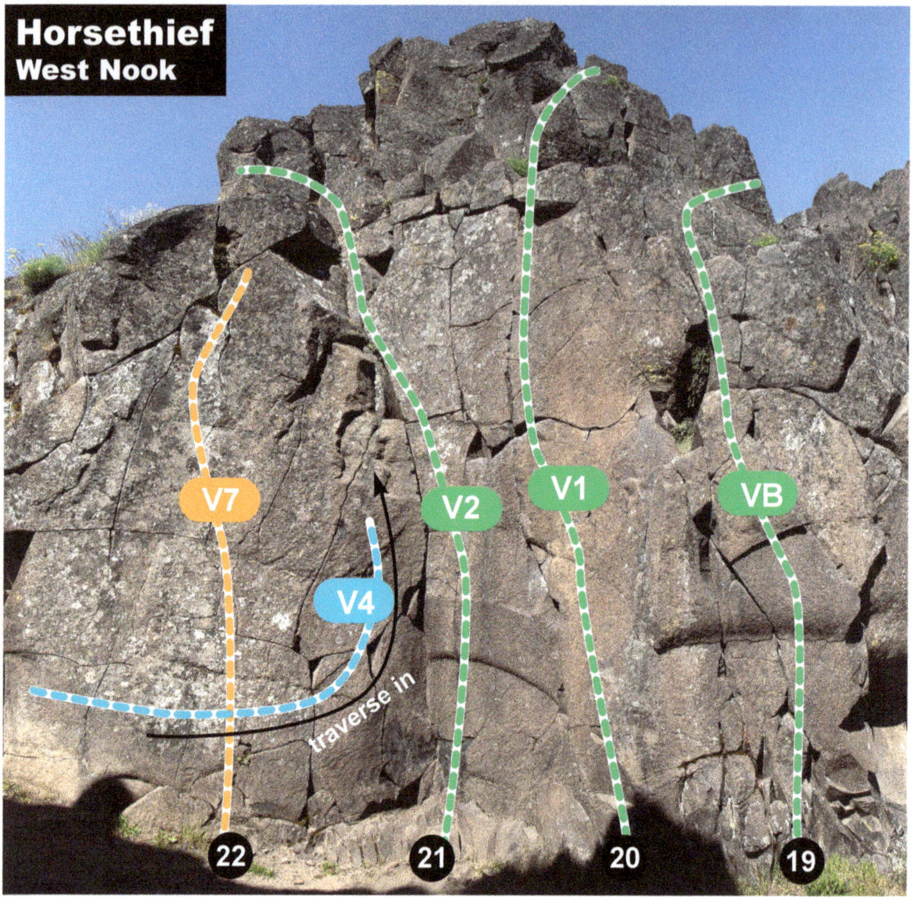

Horsethief West Nook

- V7 — 22
- V2 — 21
- V4 (traverse in)
- V1 — 20
- VB — 19

26. Arête (CLOSED)
This is the outer buttress with posted off-limits signs informing visitors of the aboriginal petroglyph graffiti.

INNER CORRIDOR

From the First Main Amphitheater walk through a small opening in the cliff scarp (The Narrows). This quickly opens up into the Main Inner Corridor or Grotto. On your immediate left is the Petroglyph Overhang and just beyond (also on the left) is the Sunny Patina. A smidge beyond on the left is the Long Alcove. If you continue walking di-

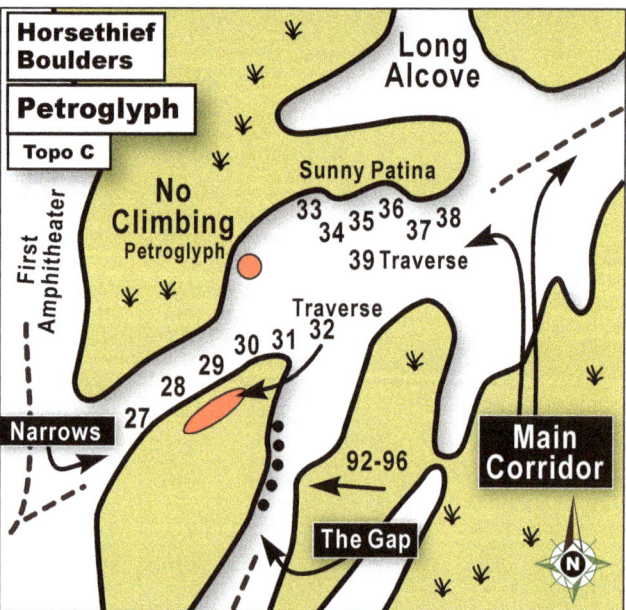

Horsethief Boulders Petroglyph Topo C

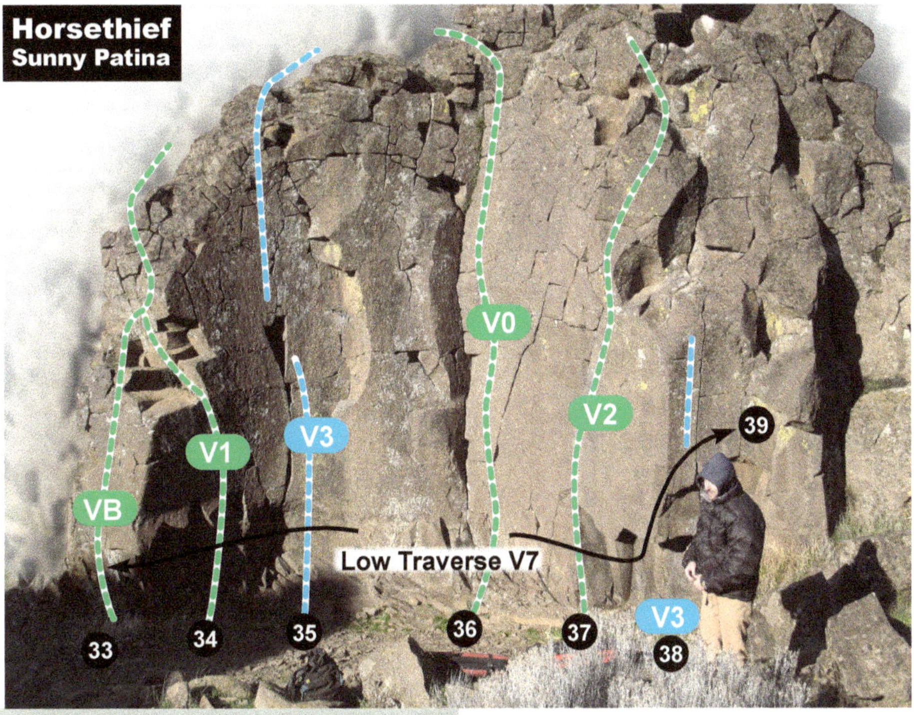

Horsethief
Sunny Patina

rectly east all the way through this Main Inner Corridor you will pass the Long Wall and exit out the East Entrance to the North Point.

The Narrows (Topo C)

The first five problems are located on the right (south) wall in The Narrows just as you are entering the Main Corridor across from the 'off-limits' sign on the opposite side of the corridor.

27. V1 Thin Crack ☐
Jam the thin crack in the corner.

28. V0 Steep Face ☐
Climb up the steep face on fractured jugs.

29. V2 Bulging Prow ☐
A minor bulge prow.

30. V3 Tall Face ★ ⚠ ☐
A very committing tall boulder problem on a fairly tall face.

31. V4 Tall Arête ★★ ⚠ ☐
A difficult line with tenuous pinches and smears on the lower half of a tall arête.

Horsethief — The Narrows South Side

Lock into each sequence, hold the balance, then slap for the rounded sloper.

Traverse Challenge
32. V3 Narrows Traverse ☐
Do a healthy traverse from before #27 passing the tall arête (#31).

PETROGLYPH OVERHANG (CLOSED) (TOPO C)

This is an overhanging inner scoop on the north side of the inner corridor at the narrows. There are posted off-limits signs informing visitors of the aboriginal petroglyphs.

Sunny Patina

After you admire the off-limits petroglyphs wander a few yards east to a great little sunny kink where this fine selection of favorites can be found. Definitely fire up the triangular shaped pocket climb called Arrow Point. In the distant past this line had a small block wedged in the triangle pocket with two ¼" bolts and a slice of metal holding it in place. Now days we all just enjoy the nature of the line without all that old hardware.

33. VB Arête ☐
Short and juggy and a little loose on top.

34. V1 Face ★ ☐
A bump problem over a slight hang on a nose. A bit loose at top.

35. V2 Arrowhead ★★★ ☐
Certainly one of the best face climbs at the Butte. Start left of the corner and balance up using the triangular arrow-like feature with your left hand. Power through a series of wild face crimper moves past the triangle, and to slightly loose jug holds at the top. Eliminates are also possible.

36. V0 Cool Corner ★★★ ☐
A classic stemming problem in the corner with a variety of small holds.

37. V1 Thin Crack ★ ☐
Two thin cracks power up away rightward from the corner. Using both thin cracks work up rightward and trick your way onto the slopers above. Eliminate bumps up grade to V2.

38. V3ss Arête ☐
Sit start at hidden undercling and ends with a mantle finish.

The **Triangle of Pain** V5 rules on this same arête. Sit start to jug undercling, left crimp, triangle crimp in middle of face, left arête, mono-pocket right of the arête, and top to a mantle.

Traverse Challenge
39. V7 Low Traverse ☐
Start on #33 and traverse right staying low to finish on top block 6' right of route #38. It is about V4 if you start on left and end high, and V7 if you start on left and end low on right.

THE LONG ALCOVE (TOPO D)

Walking east along the Main Inner Corridor (or Grotto) past the Petroglyph Overhang you will find a Long Alcove running left (north). This long alcove splits into two directions; the longer portion continuing north while the Veranda cuts back hard west to a very popular cul-de-sac.

The Veranda

The Veranda is a stellar slice on the immediate left in the Long Alcove. This north facing and very flat smooth face has become one of the most popular spots to power up. The tick-list of problems here and the quality of the rock (smooth and slippery) combine to provide a string of favorites that will keep you jumping. The first problem starts on the very nose while the remainder is on the flat, steep, north-facing shaded aspect.

40. V1 Outer Buttress ★ ☐
Crimps and stemming lead to jugs and a nice finish. Variations exist (V2/V3).

41. V1 Arête to Corner ★ ☐
Smear up ramp using a seam, palm the minor arête onto a tiny perch, then finish up a small inside corner.

42. V2 Thin Crack ★★★ ☐
Classic boulder problem, and polished from plenty of use. One of the most well-known Horsethief problems.

43. V3 Thin Face ★★★ ☐
Start on lowest holds 5' up for V3 rating. A

Veranda / Long Alcove • GB 97

Horsethief
Veranda

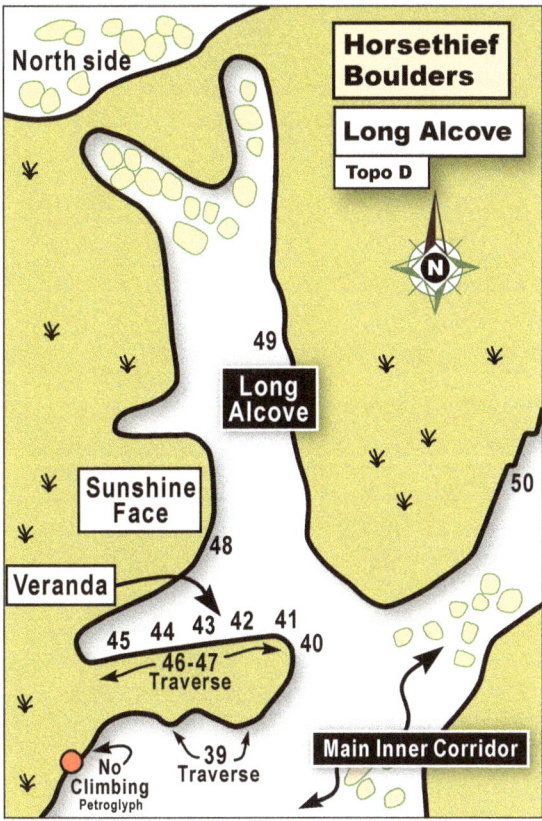

Horsethief Boulders
Long Alcove
Topo D

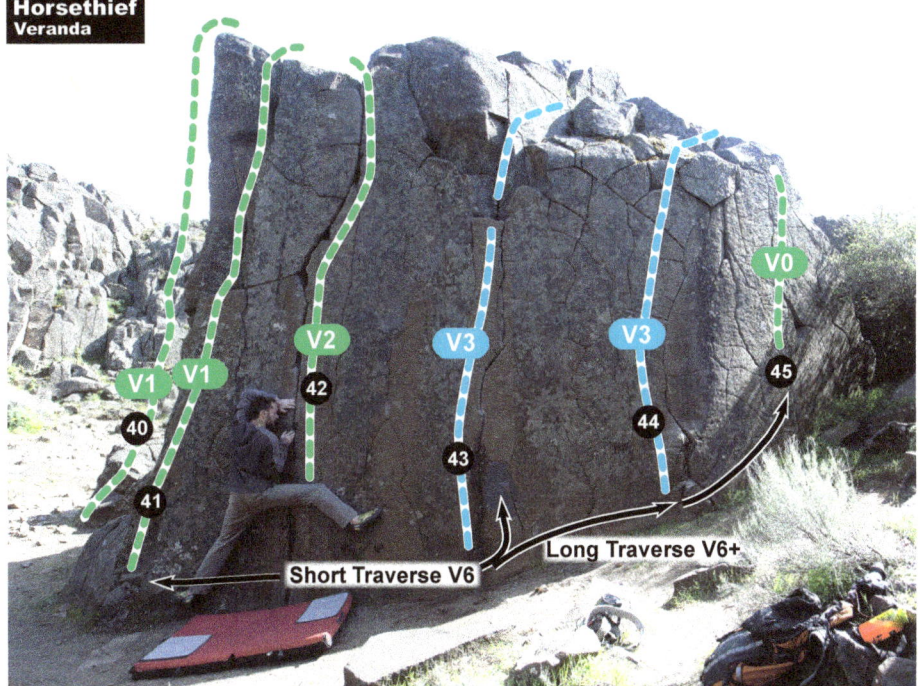

Short Traverse V6
Long Traverse V6+

Horsethief test-piece.

44. V3 Face ★ ☐

Avoid the good jug on the right or the problem will be easier still.

45. V0 Face ☐

Right most very short problem. The finishing block seems kind of sketchy.

TRAVERSE CHALLENGE

46. V7 Long Traverse ☐

Start on Arête (#41) and traverse low for the full length of wall, ending on the top of down climb rocks after Face (#45) and ends at the bush.

47. V6 Short Traverse ☐

Start on Thin Crack (#41) and traverse right to Face (#43) and finish up to the top on that route.

Sunshine Face ⚠

In the Long Alcove is this sunny slice of rock which faces southeast and offers several top-rope problems of moderate difficulty on a nice wide and tall section of wall.

48. VB Sunshine Face ★ ☐

Plenty of variables on a steep tall hi-ball face if you are comfortable with height (5.6 to 5.9). The base of the cliff even has a few V2-V4 eliminate problems if it catches your eye just right.

East Face of Long Alcove ⚠

Walk deeper into this Long Alcove until you are surrounded by poison oak bushes. On your left (west) side of the long alcove is a viable narrow minor arête with a thin left crack and edge-like features. On the right (east) side of the long alcove several fine long lead or top-rope climbs are available with plenty of variations, so do not feel limited to the only

Bouldering at the *Veranda*

East Inner Corridor / Classic Arête

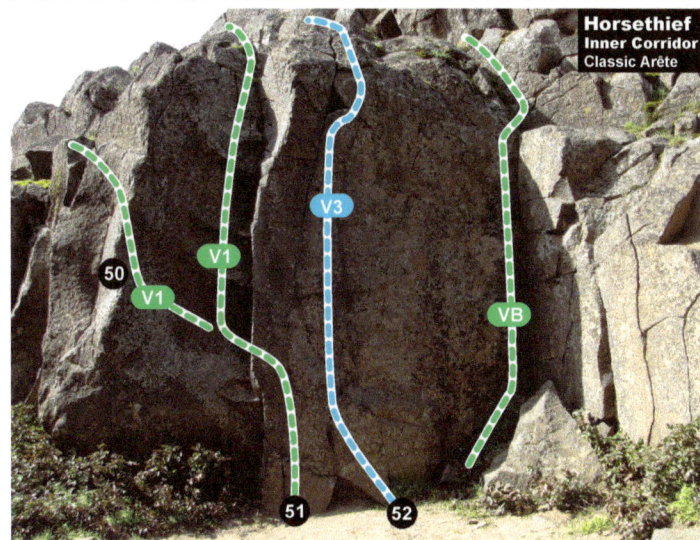

Horsethief
Inner Corridor
Classic Arête

over-aged hillbilly listed below.

49. VB Crack Corner ★ ☐
The obvious tall crack (5.7) and corner climb (multiple exits) on east wall of the Long Alcove.

EAST HALF OF INNER CORRIDOR

Walk further east along the Main Corridor beyond the Long Alcove. The Classic Arête is located on the sunny north side at a kink, while the ever popular Long Wall is on the shaded south side of the Corridor. At the far east end of the Main Corridor you will see the East Grotto Face, while beyond is the East Exit/entrance that quickly leads over to the North Point.

The Classic Arête

The next three problems are on a stellar sunny steep flat face with a prominent crisp short arête. Working the arête is one of the finest problems at the Butte. I never knew that V1 could be so fun till I tried this one. Nice sandy landing.

50. V1 Dull Prow ☐
A minor round prow as a left exit.

51. V1 Sharp Arête ★★★ ☐
Use the sharp arête and gingerly slide up left into the inside corner, and then dance up on intricate small edges to the large incut hold at the top. Classic Horsethief boulder problem.

52. V3 Seam Only ★★ ☐
Avoid arête on the left at this grade. Involves a long lock-off to a mono-pocket, and then to a jug hold (wobbles but still there).

Long Wall (Topo E) ⚠

The Long Wall is one of the most popular sections of wall at the Butte. This portion of wall faces north and on hot days stays shaded while offering a plethora of fine problems, including one of the best traverses at the Butte. Most of the problems on the Long Wall are hi-ball.

Many of the climbs along the Long Wall offer numerous variables, so rather than attempting to solve every idiosyncratic nuance…just start with the short easier problems then gradually expand your options.

53. V2 Face to Mantle ☐
Immediately south of the Long Alcove on the shaded Long Wall. Down climb off right immediately after the mantle.

54. VB Thin Crack ★ ☐
The striking thin crack (5.8) with good pure jamming, but it's short lived.

55. VB Green Slab ☐
A long green slab with many variations (5.6 to 5.9); some are harder while some are easier.

56. V1 (V3ss) Short Overhang ☐

100 HORSETHIEF BOULDERS • The Long Wall

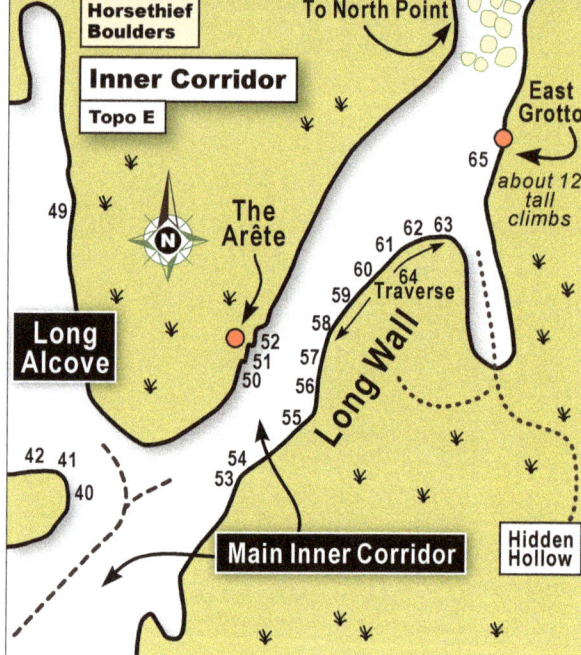

Start sitting, do the overhang, and end on a ledge. Or stand start and make it V1 fun.

57. VB Corner to Ledge ★

Climb the shallow inside corner to an awkward move getting on the big flat ledge (5.7) then waltz up the right face to top out.

58. VB Face to Groove ★★

Great line! Climb the steep face (5.8) on good holds to finish up a lower angled groove.

59. V0 Steep Face ★★★

Super classic line. Start at the thin crack and climb up an awkward face past missing blocks.

60. VB Face to Groove ★★

Climb up the enjoyable well-feature face (5.7) that has lots of cracks and holds until it eases in difficulty in the groove to the top. Beware of a loose thin flake up high.

61. VB Face ★
Steep face with sequential holds (5.8).

62. VB Thin Block ★
Grab the long thin block (5.7) and climb up to a big edge and finish on the lower angle rock.

63. VB Groove
A moderate groove (5.5) on good rock at the far left end of Long Wall prior to the uphill scramble.

TRAVERSE CHALLENGE

64. V3-V6 Long Wall Traverse ★★
A totally stellar boulder traverse can be done along the Long Wall in either direction. Start just west of Corner to Ledge #57 and continue

East Grotto / North Point • GB 101

Horsethief
Inner Corridor
East Grotto Face

to Groove #63. About V6 if staying low for the entire traverse. Or pick a shorter distance for a techy V3. This traverse is the reason to be at Horsethief. A superb boulder problem!

East Grotto Face ⚠

A nice sunny slab. The rounded slab formation is less than vertical and has many cracks and seams crisscrossing the face at angles.

65. VB-V0 Face ★ ☐
Nice blocky climbing on a wide rounded face with a corner in the middle of the wall (variations from 5.7 to 5.10-).

North Point (Topo F) ⚠

The following three routes are quite tall (roped stuff only) and are located at a sharp prow of rock facing out over the East Entrance. Most climbers reach this locale by walking through the entire inner main corridor. This info is just for reference and not intended that you should boulder solo this stuff.

66. V1 Old Bolt Crack ☐
Cruises up a smooth vertical face (several old ¼" bolts studs) past an upside down triangle roof feature on a flat patina face (5.10-). Once you power past the triangle into the thin jam crack to a stance, continue up easy steps in a corner to the top. Somewhat loose at the top.

66b. VB Jug Haul ★ ☐
About 30' left of #66 route is a nice short (5.9) jug haul boulder problem on a flat face.

67. V0 North Point Crack ★ ☐
Climb a steep crack to a stance, and then climb a smear move into a corner system immediately left of the arête (5.10b).

68. V3 North Point Arête ★ ☐
Start at the North Crack and launch up right (2 bolts) on a smooth face, and then power out (3 bolts) the severely overhung (5.11c) arête to the top.

West Entrance (Topo G) ⚠

There are several options near the West Entrance path that are good for learning technique. One notable section is on the left as you proceed up the incline into the First Amphitheater (the Nook & Tier zone) alongside the path (see Topo G). Offers a brief compact selection of short VB-V4 problems.

69. VB West Chimney ☐
The West Chimney (5.4) is found at the very tip of the West Point, and is a nice chimney smack between the main wall and a large obvious isolated pillar. Stem the chimney to the top of the pillar, and then launch up the nice series of steps and ledges to the tip of West Point. Once you top out on the tip you can easily descend southward down a boulder field slope. Or you can continue up another short steep step onto the main upper plateau and

walk east to descend into the First Amphitheater.

78. VB Tall Crack Corner
A fairly well-used corner climb (5.6) is available to your immediate south as you are hiking up the slope of the West Entrance.

South Wall (Topo H)

To reach the South Wall river face hike past the Western Entrance south eastward around the Butte until you can see an obvious isolated pillar separate from the main massif. Scramble up a boulder slope to the base of the west-facing slot formed by this isolated pillar. These two climbs are on the main wall just to the left of the slot. These are a bit too tall for bouldering and are for reference here only.

81. V0 Corner & Roof ⚠
A good long climb and best done as a toprope. Climb a steep corner and power out the overhang directly to the top.

82. VB Face and Prow ⚠
Begin by powering up left (5.9) using the prow and nearby features and continue to the top.

Hidden Hollow (Topo I, J, K)

A quality string of short problems on a rock plateau south of the inner corridor. To reach it, ascend up a big stepped slot from the Inner Corridor at the Long Wall that land on a scenic plateau, then drop down into another low grassy dell.

NORTH SIDE - HIDDEN HOLLOW

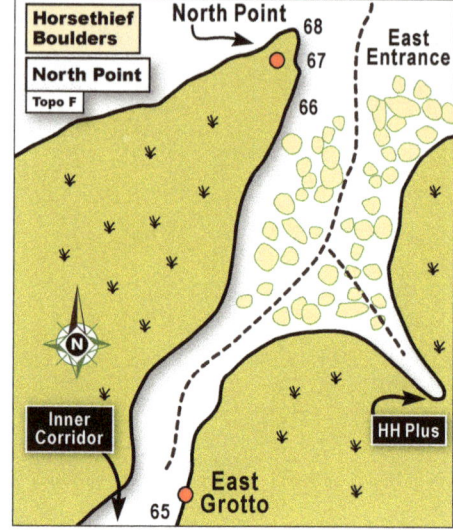

The beta details for the north side problems, L to R (West to East).

97. VBss High Jug
Begin on low horizontal, then power up over high nose.

98. V0ss Crack
Climb the crack.

99. VBss OW Arête
Climb the face with right hand on the arête. The arête has a deep offwidth crack behind it.

100. V4ss Outer Point
Climb the outer point.

101. V6ss Arête ★
A slightly overhung tall flat-face with a sharp

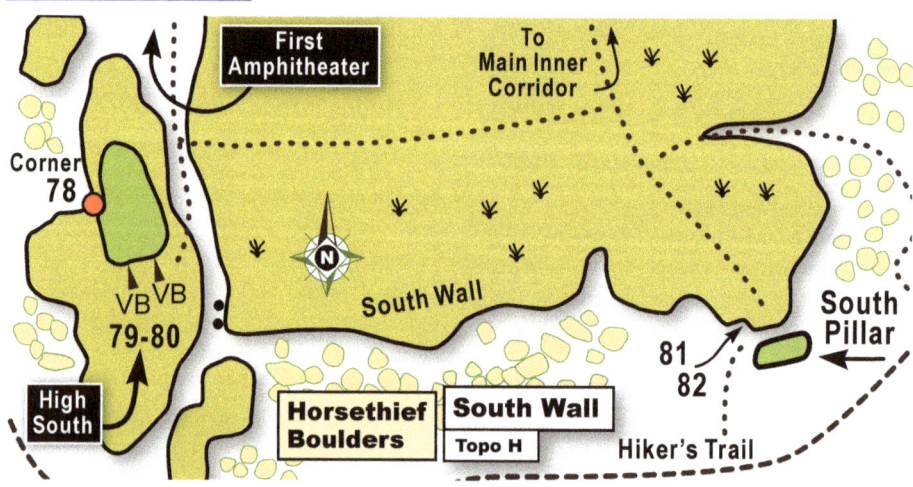

Hidden Hollow / HH+ • GB 103

outer edge on the lower left. Sit start on crimps with left initially low on outer edge. Crimps mid-face, yet hs better exits holds up high.

102. V4ss Face ☐
Thin crimps on a slightly hung face.

Crack 'n Face Cluster:

This is located about 20' right of the main string of problems.

103. V3ss Low Bulge ☐
At east end of Hidden Hollow. Sit start a short low bulging overhang using just the round arête.

104. V2ss Crack/Face ☐
A short crack corner that is overhung. Climb mostly the deep V-shaped crack corner.

105. V0ss Shorty ☐
Shorty round bulge with crimps.

SOUTH SIDE - HIDDEN HOLLOW
The beta details for the south side problems, left to right (East to West).

106. V1 Outer Arête ☐
Climb the left-leaning arête of wide flat face. Left hand is on arête, right on crimps.

107. V0 Face ☐
Numerous thin cracks and edges crisscross at angles on a nice wide flat face.

108. V0ss Jugs ☐
Jugs on a short face.
A gap of about 30' to next problems.

109. VBss Jugs ☐
Jugs on a short flat face.

110. V2ss Crimps ☐
Short low sit start using crimps and left prow, but marginal

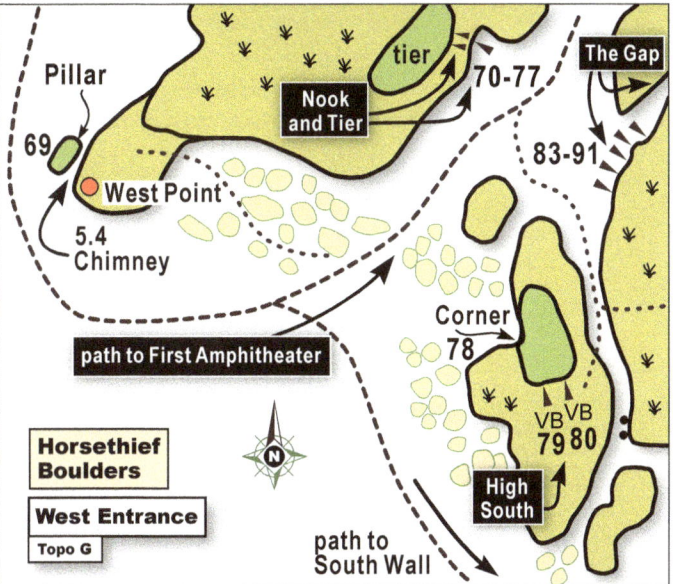

smears for feet.

Hidden Hollow Plus

From the main Hidden Hollow walk northeast about 100' into another low grassy hollow (HH Plus Extension) where you will find another brief fine series of quality boulder problems ranging from VB to V3 (some are hi-ball). See topo K.

HH PLUS PART 1

In the first low grassy vale, the beta is left to right.

111. VB Shorty Face ☐
Minor short flat face.

112. V0 Classic Arete ☐

The obvious classic right angling jug arête.

113. V_ Hi-ball face
Quality hi-ball face beckons.

114. VB Corner crack

115. VB Basic
The rightmost basic line.

116. VB Juggy Bulge
Juggy bulge fun run located on the east side of this little vale across from the first problem.

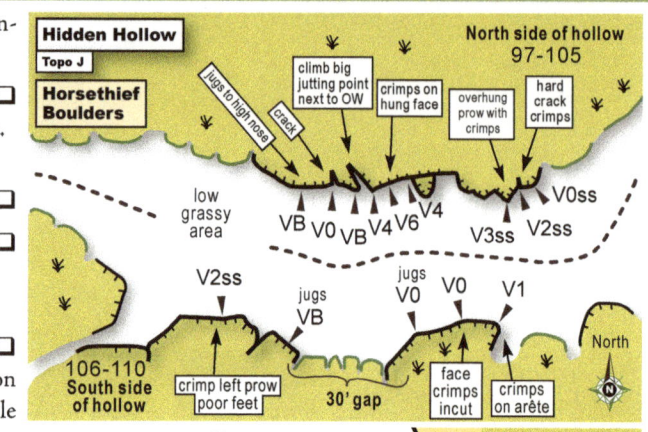

HH Plus - Part 2
A set of problems at the narrowest part of this slot (before it spills out onto a talus field in the general vicinity of the North Point). Most of the problems are on the right (east) side of this narrow slot. Beta is described right to left.

117. V0 Incuts & Jug
Classic hung incuts and jugs fun run.

118. V2/V3 Tall Corner
Quality tall corner with thin holds and smears.

119. V2/V3 Tall Prow
A tall prow with small holds, but it beckons.

120. V_ Crack
Tall crack that also beckons.

And a final problem on the left side of slot:

121. V3ss Nothing
Some kind of short nothing on the left side of this narrow slot zone.

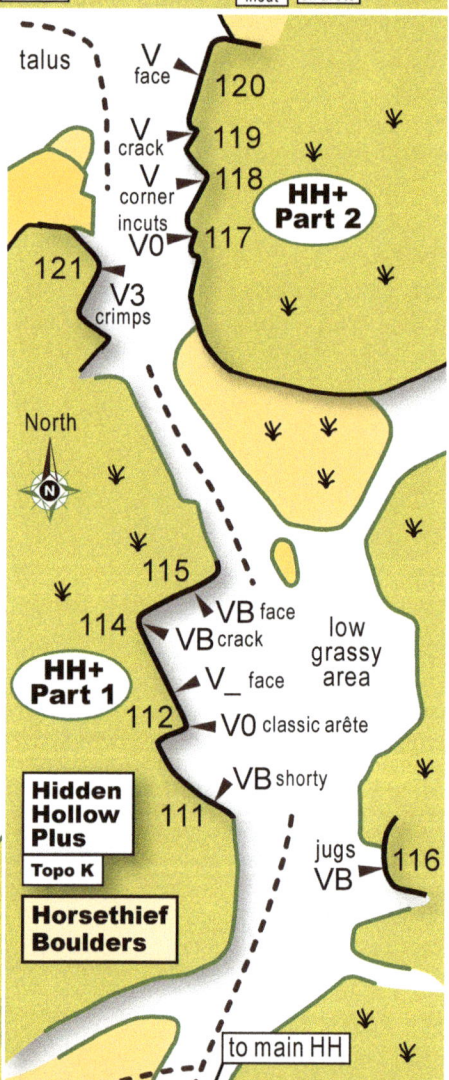

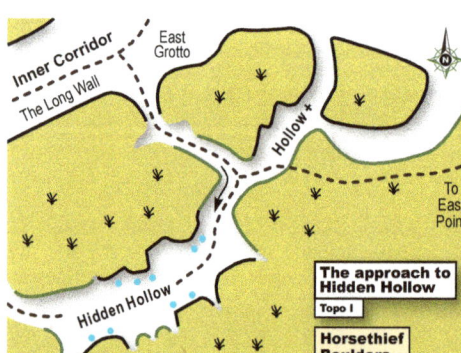

Stellar Gem Quality Bouldering

5

HUNCHBACK BOULDERS

The Hunchback Boulders are nestled quietly in a tantalizing tall Douglas fir forest which invites boulderer's to experience a little andesite bouldering near the elusive mega wall known as the Hunckback Wall. A gentle forest breeze generally keeps the place at a comfortable temperature even on hot summer days. This is a place where the sounds of nature predominate.

The problems range from VB to V8 (to date), are generally limited in totality mainly because there are only three boulders. The largest is of behemoth size (30' x 18') with a serious overhang on two aspects. The ultra cool main mega-stone has about 15 lines (one aspect is a superb 30' long traverse with a 45° undercut). Both nearby smaller stones have been tapped as well. Just 1-2 crashpads recommended, no ticks, no poison oak, good cell reception, low altitude (2400'), season from May-Oct, and sometimes accessible even into the winter months (if it's dry).

The site has a convenient proximity to Portland (1-hour drive) with paved road access to the parking spot. A 25-minute steep uphill grunt on a narrow path gets you to the boulders, though due to the stout uphill grunt hike from the road it may keep some individuals at bay.

History: First tapped into by Mr O (2016); yet many of the superb quality powerful V-grades were tapped by the famous Abbott/Anglin team shortly thereafter in 2018.

DIRECTIONS

Drive east on U.S. Hwy 26 from Sandy, Oregon till you reach Welches. Turn south at the Subway store onto Salmon River Road (NF 2618). Continue about 9/10 mile south passing a guardrail on the right, a small rotten roadside bluff on the left, and a deeply cut ravine also on the left. Park immediately on the west side of the road at a minor pullout. Step into the dry ravine for a few yards, then angle up right onto the south slope into a grove of cedar trees. A faint path begins there and zigzags gently uphill, and gradually steepens for the remainder of the uphill hike (see diagram).

Hunchback Boulder

STELLAR WEST OVERHANG

The following problems are on the superb quality overhung west aspect (the beta is described right to left):

1. V3 Of Noble Birth ★★★ ❏
Jug start. The rightmost line. Grab jug, move up right on crimps, turning a lip onto the slab. Good warmup.

2. V5ss Noble Birth Extension ★★★★ ❏
The 'ss' extension of the above line. Sit low to ground then bump to jug, then continue up right around lip.

3. V5 Bell Ringer ★★ ❏
High crimp start. Start on high crimp, punch to lip and get over quickly.

4. V6 Bell Ringer (standing) ★★★ ❏
Standing start on big jug, then straight up to lip and over onto slab.

5. V7ss Bell Ringer ★★★★ ❏
Stellar full deal low traverse. Start on low fat rail, move right, then directly up to jug, then

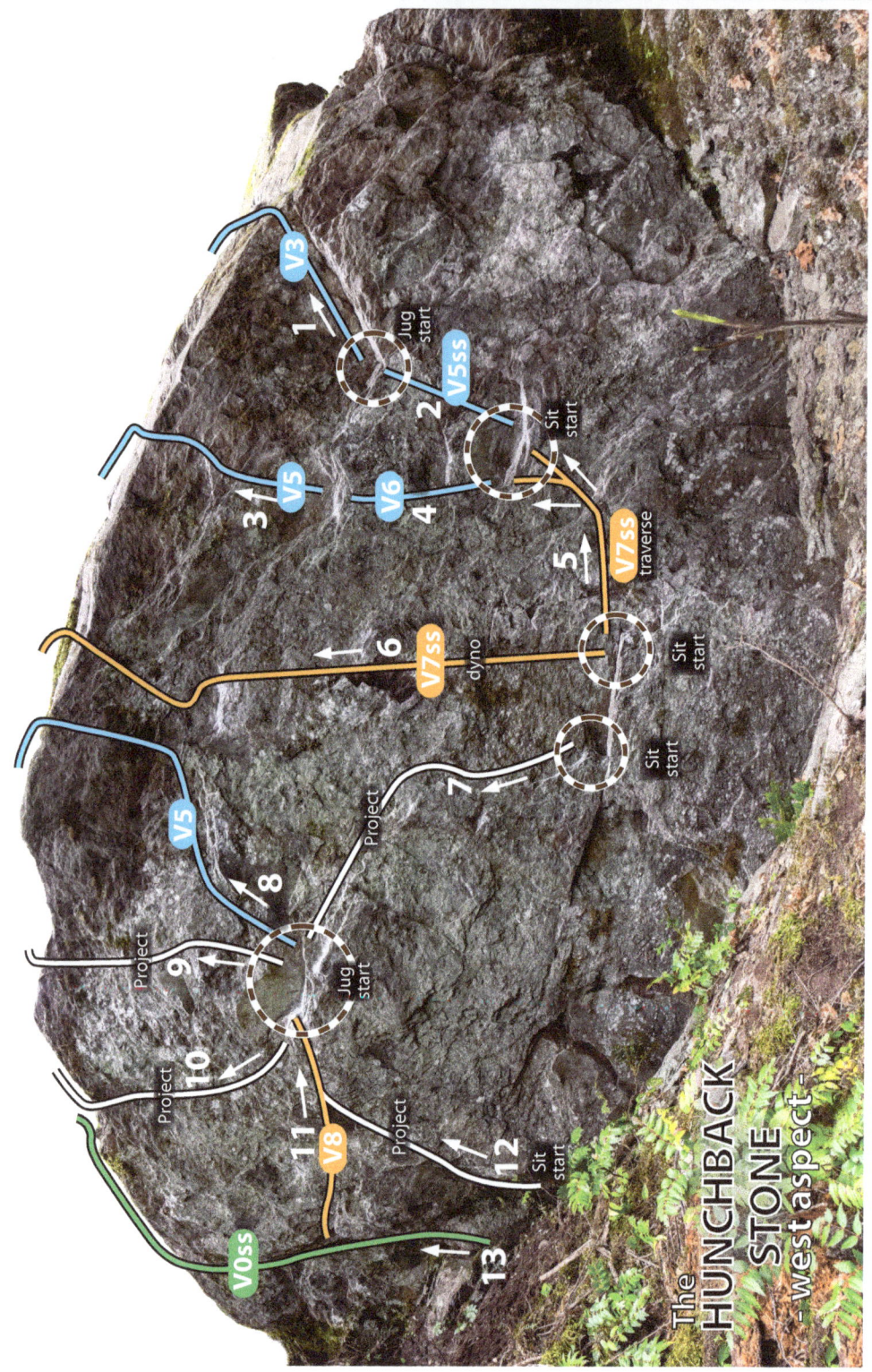

crimps to lip and over the lip onto slab.

6. V7ss Acceptable Losses ★ ★ ★ ★
Dyno straight up. Start on low fat rail, and do a full on dyno to snag the high jug.

7. V7-9 [?] _____
Start on low fat rail, and fire crimps up left to merge into the Full Moto (project).

8. V5 Quasi Moto ★ ★ ★
High jug start, up right on crimps to lip, then over lip onto slab.

9. V__ _____
From same high jug but straight up (project).

10. V__ _____
From same high jug but up left (project).

11. V8ss Full Moto. ★ ★ ★ ★
Sit start on Megalonia, then run thin crimps right to reach a high jug, then go up right to lip (using the Quasi Moto ending).

12. V__ _____
A potential thin crimps direct line starting low next to Megalonia (project).

13. V0ss Megalonia ★ ★ ★ ★
The leftmost line. Layback hung crack, then along the lip on jugs rightward, then do a mantle move onto slab. Great warmup.

SOUTH ASPECT

Beta is described from left to right (lower to upper) on the south aspect on the boulder. All the routes land on a low angle slab:

1. VB Imperialism ★
The basic up/down. Step up onto block, then move up left to center rib and go up to top.

2. VB Liquid Desire ★
Face variation. Step up onto the slab, but just before the center rib cruise a brief low angle slab face.

3. VB Royalty ★ ★

Crimps on a low angle slab. Step up onto the stone, and immediately go directly up a thin edge slab with nice crimps.

4. V2 Exploited Class ★ ★
Surmount an overhung lip (mantle) onto the slab then join the previous problem to finish.

5. V2 Ruling Class ★ ★ ★ ★
Unique rock hole. Surmount overhang (mantle). Then climb directly up slab to top.

6. V_ss [?] _____
Viable overhung optional sit start (project).

7. V3 (V_ss) Lemming Lore ★ ★
Overhung crimp pulls at a slight notch in the rock face. Then a few crimp moves on the steep slab to top out.

8. V4 (V_ss) The Abyss
A well overhung thuggish prow.

9. VB Noob
Just a fat dirty slot, used generally to get down.

THE TRAVERSE:

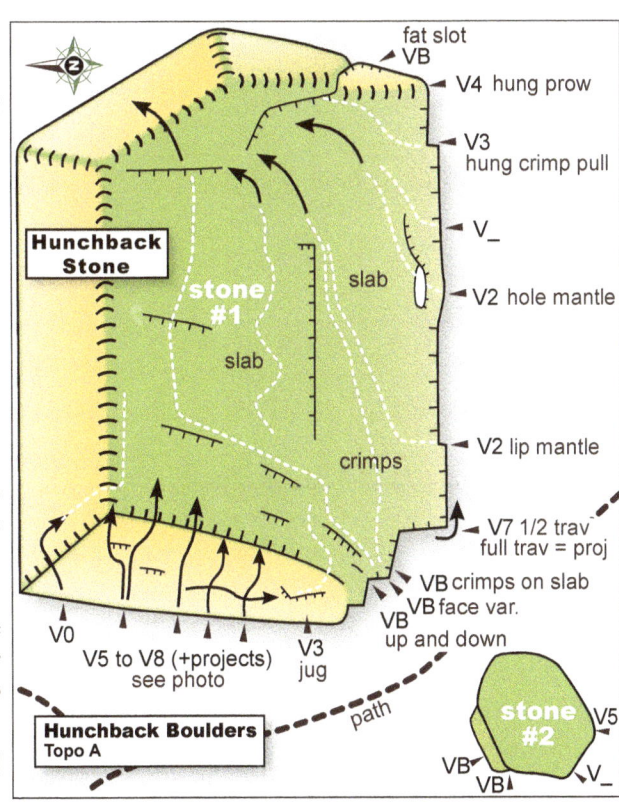

108 ADDITIONAL SITE OPTIONS • Hunchback Boulders

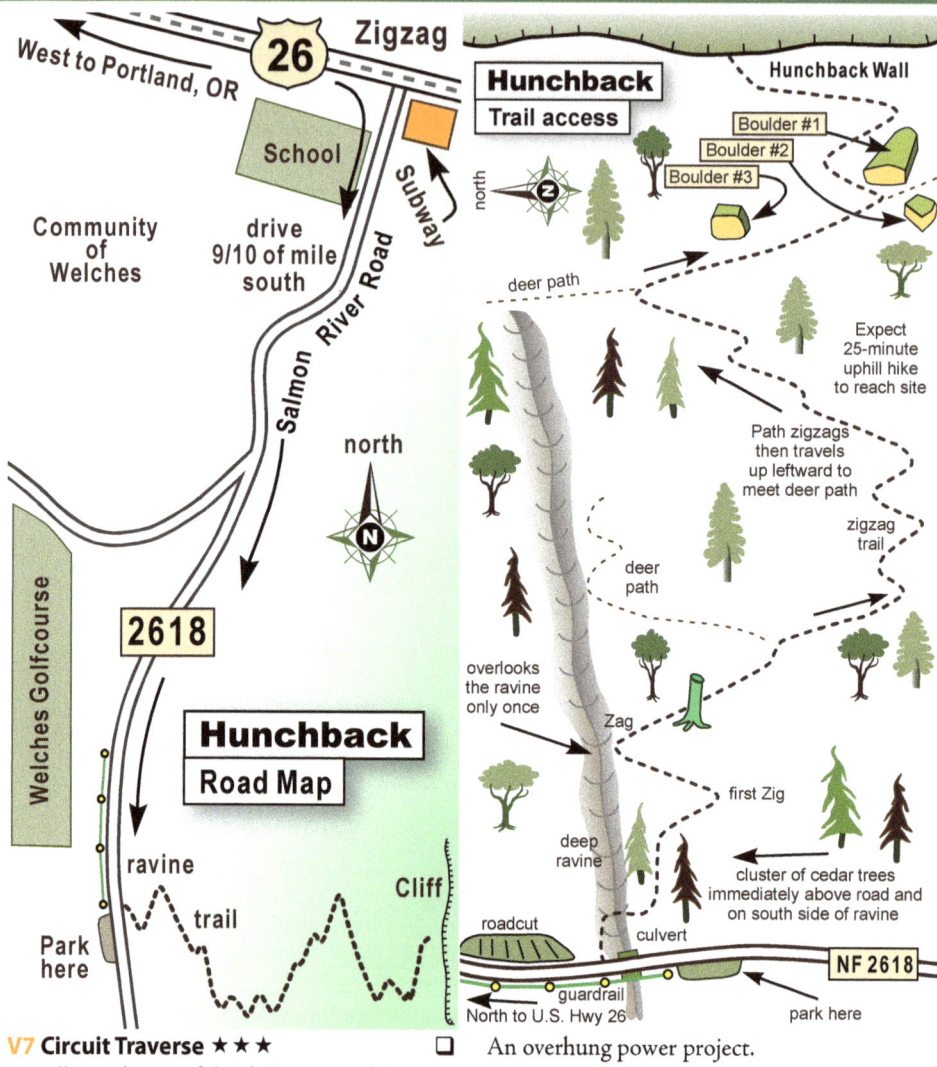

V7 Circuit Traverse ★★★
A stellar and powerful uphill traverse (the lower ½ is done). Involves round sloped holds, heel hooks, along a substantially undercut hanging traverse.

Quasimodo Boulder

Just a few yards to the SW of the big boulder is this unique little boulder. Beta is listed from left to right):

VB _____
A brief short flat face.

VB _____
Brief set of sloped outer steps.

V_ (?)
An overhung power project.

V5 Ex Libris ★★★
The rightmost hung crimps power line (the 'ss' is about V7ss).

Esmeralda Boulder

A minor boulder located about 100' to the north of the main big Hunchback boulder along the trail (you pass it en route to the main boulder). Beta is listed right to left:

V2 Zeno's ★
A short rounded face (use right hand on rib), then power a few moves onto a small perch.

V2 Esmeralda ★
A thin groove seam rounds quickly to a small

slab stance. Exit right (south).

V7/8 ❏
Left center face starting on crimps, but as it rounds onto a slab the holds virtually vanish.

V5/6 Ab Antiquo ❏
The leftmost rounded nose with flat crimps going up onto a small slab.

www.ingramcontent.com/pod-product-compliance
Lightning Source LLC
Chambersburg PA
CBHW051550010526
44118CB00022B/2652